How Children
Acquire "Academic"
Skills Without
Formal Instruction

How Children Acquire "Academic" Skills Without Formal Instruction

PETER GRAY

TIPPING POINTS PRESS
The Alliance for Self-Directed Education
CAMBRIDGE, MA, USA

Published by Tipping Points Press
The Alliance for Self-Directed Education

First paperback edition published in 2020 by Tipping Points Press

ISBN: 978-1-952837-04-3 (paperback)
ISBN: 978-1-952837-05-0 (ebook)

Library of Congress Cataloging-in-Publication Data
Names: Gray, Peter, author.
Title: How Children Acquire "Academic" Skills Without Formal Instruction
Description: Tipping Points Press, The Alliance for Self-Directed Education
    [2020] | Includes biographical references and index.
Subjects: Alternative education, Cognitive-developmental theory, Self-
    direction (psychology).
Identifiers: ISBN 978-1-952837-04-3 (paperback) |
    ISBN 978-1-952837-05-0 (ebook)

The chapters published in this book were previously published as separate articles in Peter Gray's column, "Freedom to Learn" in *Psychology Today* and are presented here with permission.

Cover Illustration Credit: Karin Stankušová
Cover & Interior Design Credit: Elliott Beard

Contents

Editor's Preface

Myriad thinkers before our time have diagnosed the ills of conventional educational systems and prescribed their cures. Dr. Peter Gray's magnificent contributions to this vital field, however, transcend the familiar routine of pointing out problems and proposing new methods to replace them. He rightly reframes the issue in the broader terms of civil liberties—in particular, the rights of children—and identifies the primary need for young people to take back their childhood. Peter has spent a remarkable 36-year career researching the relationship children have historically had with play and learning in their societies since the time of hunters and gatherers. In doing so, he has established a broad, humanitarian view of childhood that counteracts our culture's myopic, impersonal focus on assessment and workforce training. This compendium of essays, categorized by subject, catalogues the complete thoughts thus far of Dr. Gray's research on the importance of childhood freedom.

Peter's research and writing have made significant impacts on diverse populations concerned with the wellbeing and education of children, shifting his readers' thinking on children's rights and their understanding of what childhood has looked like over the history of humankind. I have heard innumerable firsthand accounts of the effect of Peter's work on parents, educators, play advocates, young people, and youth rights activists ranging from Sub-Saharan Africa to the Baltic States and from East Asia to South America. For example, a mother in Greece told me how Peter's writing motivated her to withdraw her child from the local school system and start a democratic education movement. A Sudbury school struggling to open in Turkey, where Self-Directed Education is illegal, attested to me that his writing inspired them to try it despite the risk and difficulty. A teenager in the U.S. Midwest attributed Peter's writing as the foundation of her effort to drop out of school and become an unschooler.

This begs the question, what is it about Dr. Gray's insightful research and writing that universally seems to inspire a new generation to risk breaking with convention and to actualize freedom through education, parenting, and personal growth? I cannot speak for all, but I think I may have an inkling. Peter's experience as a research professor of evolutionary, developmental, and educational psychology gives him an advantageous perspective on the subject of child rearing and learning. He is able to draw his readers out of society's normative obsession with assessment and workforce productivity, and compel us to pursue the deeper question of "What is it all for?" He backs up his perspectives with primary research, valid scientific evidence, and detailed explanations of the long history of self-directed childhoods.

In his 2013 book, *Free to Learn: Why Unleashing the Instinct to Play Will Make Our Children Happier, More Self-Reliant, and Better Students for Life*, Dr. Gray grounds his views in rigorous evolutionary research on the universal ways in which indigenous hunters and gatherers raised their young. His analysis shows that children are healthiest and learn most effectively when they are left to playfully explore their natural curiosities in a nurturing environment equipped with the tools of their culture. Dr. Gray observes that for hundreds of thousands of years, constituting nearly all of human history, this was the way in which children were raised. In other words, our species has survived throughout nearly all of our history by being trustful parents, and allowing children to self direct their own childhoods. This realization has given me, and many others, the knowledge and courage to depart and divest from the unnatural, unhealthy, and unjust attitude toward childhood that prevails in most cultures today.

Peter Gray's dedication and contribution to the subject of children's rights has inspired a new generation of advocates, now equipped with his scientific evidence of what is the long-established, just, and healthy way for children to thrive in their development. This compendium of essays, assembled and adapted from his column "Freedom to Learn," appearing in *Psychology Today*, presents the many years of findings and reporting of Dr. Gray's lifelong work. It is a contemporary reader's great fortune to have this compilation available for inspiration and documentation. And it is my great honor to provide you with this work, which also initiates a hopefully long tradition of forthcoming books about the rights of the child. This compendium marks the inaugural publication of Tipping Points Press, dedicated to the advocacy of children's rights, by the Alliance for Self-Directed Education, which Peter Gray helped to found. We look forward to the continuation of pushing forward in advocating for children's rights until we reach that tipping point, when all children are free.

Alexander Khost
Editor-in-Chief
Tipping Points Press
The Alliance for Self-Directed Education
APRIL 18, 2020

Author's Preface

I have been writing a blog for *Psychology Today* magazine, called "Freedom to Learn," since July, 2008. I have been posting there, at a rate of roughly one per month, articles dealing with child development and education, especially with children's natural ways of educating themselves when they are free to do so.

Over the years I have received many requests, from readers, for bound collections of these articles, arranged by topic, which would make the articles easier to find and easier to give to others than is possible by searching the *Psychology Today* online contents. Now, in collaboration with Tipping Points Press, the new book-publishing arm of the Alliance for Self-Directed Education (ASDE), I am responding to that request.

We are beginning with four collections, published simultaneously. The collection you have in hand is about how children acquire academic skills (especially literacy and numeracy) when allowed to do so in their own ways. The other collections in this set deal, respectively, with the harm to children that is perpetrated by our system of compulsory schooling; the evidence that Self-Directed Education works (that children in charge of their own education educate themselves well); and the natural, biological drives that underlie children's self-education and the conditions that optimize those drives. The essays have in some cases been modified slightly from the original *Psychology Today* versions, for clarity and to add more recent information.

I thank Rachel Wallach for her excellent, volunteer work in copyediting this collection; Karin Stankušová, who is a young person engaged in Self-Directed Education, for creating the cover illustration; and Alexander Khost, Editor-in-Chief of Tipping Point Press, for making these collections possible. I also thank the editors of *Psychology Today* for their support over the years in my posting these articles.

All profits from the sales of this book and others in the set help support ASDE in its mission to make opportunities for Self-Directed Education available to all families that seek it.

Peter Gray

1

Children Teach Themselves to Read

*The unschoolers' account of how
children learn to read*

FEBRUARY 24, 2010

The general assumption in our culture is that children must
be taught to read. Vast amounts of research have gone into
trying to figure out the scientifically best way to do this. In the
education stacks of any major university library you can find
rows and rows of books and many journals devoted solely to
the topic of how to teach reading. In education circles heated
debates—dubbed "the reading wars"—have raged for decades
between those who believe that most emphasis should be
placed on teaching phonics and those who take what is called
a "whole language" approach to reading instruction. Many
controlled experiments have been conducted comparing one
instruction method to another, with kindergartners and first-
graders as the guinea pigs. The phonics people say that their

method has "won" in those experiments, and the whole language people say that the experiments were rigged.

The evidence from the standard schools is that reading does not come easily to kids. Huge amounts of time and effort go into teaching reading, from preschool on through most of the elementary school years. In addition, educators encourage parents of young children to teach reading at home in order to prepare the children for reading instruction in school or to supplement that instruction. Large industries have developed around the creation and marketing of instructional materials for this purpose. There is no end to interactive computer programs, videos, and specially sequenced books designed—"scientifically," according to their proponents—to teach phonics and provide a growing base of sight words for beginning readers.

I recently read an article by two cognitive scientists (Rose & Dalton, 2009) claiming that the next development in reading instruction is going to be individualized instruction. According to the authors, modern brain imaging methods will be used to figure out the unique learning style of each child, and digital text-delivery programs will be used to teach reading to each child according to his or her unique needs and way of learning. The authors claim that they and their colleagues are, indeed, working on developing such systems. To me, this seems silly. The unique needs of each child, as they affect learning to read, are not just functions of differences in brain hardware, but vary from day to day and moment to moment based on the child's specific experiences, wishes, and whims, which the child himself or herself controls. I'll begin to believe these researchers' claims when I see evidence that brain imaging can be used to predict, in advance, the contents of daydreams.

In marked contrast to all this frenzy about teaching reading stands the view of people involved in the unschooling and democratic schooling movements, who claim that reading need not be taught at all! As long as kids grow up in a literate society, surrounded by people who read, they will learn to read. They may ask some questions along the way and get a few pointers from others who already know how to read, but they will take the initiative in all of this and orchestrate the entire process themselves. This is individualized learning, but it does not require brain imaging or cognitive scientists, and it requires little effort on the part of anyone other than the child who is learning. Each child knows intuitively what his or her own learning style is and what he or she is ready for, and will learn to read in his or her own unique way, on his or her unique schedule.

Twenty-one years ago two of my undergraduate students conducted a study of how students learn to read at the Sudbury Valley School, where students are free all day to do as they wish (for more on Sudbury Valley, see Gray, 2008, or visit the school's website). They identified 16 students who had learned how to read after enrolling in the school and had received no systematic reading instruction, and they interviewed the students, their parents, and school staff to try to figure out when, why, and how each of them learned to read. What they found defied every attempt at generalization. Students began their first real reading at a remarkably wide range of ages—from as young as 4 to as old as 14. Some students learned very quickly, going from apparently complete non-reading to fluent reading in a matter of weeks; others learned much more slowly. A few learned in a conscious manner, systematically working on phonics and asking for help along the way. Others just "picked it up." They realized, one day, that they could read, but they had no idea how they had learned to do so. There was no systematic relationship between the age at which students had first learned to read and their involvement with reading at the time of the interview. Some of the most voracious readers had learned early and others had learned late.

My son, who is a staff member at Sudbury Valley, tells me that that study is now out of date. His impression is that most Sudbury Valley students today are learning to read earlier, and with even less conscious effort than before, because they are immersed in a culture in which people are communicating regularly with the written word—in computer games, email, Facebook, cell-phone texting, and the like. The written word is not essentially different to them from the spoken word, so the biological machinery for picking up spoken language is more or less automatically employed in their learning to read and write (or type). I'd love to study this in some way, but so far haven't figured out how to do it without being intrusive.

In January 2010, I invited readers of my *Psychology Today* blog who are involved in unschooling or Sudbury model schooling to write to me with stories about learning to read without formal instruction. Eighteen people—most of whom identified themselves as parents of unschoolers and some of whom wrote about more than one child—kindly shared their stories with me. Each story is unique. Just as my students found in their study at Sudbury Valley, there seems to be no pattern to how unschooled children today are learning to read.

By listing and organizing the main points made by each story, I did, however, extract what seem to me to be seven principles that may cast some general understanding on the process of learning to read without schooling. I have chosen to organize the remainder of this essay around these principles and to exemplify each with quotations from stories that were sent to me. Some of the people who sent stories asked that I use only their first names and not their children's names, so I will use that convention throughout.

Seven Principles of Learning to Read Without Schooling

1. For non-schooled children there is no critical period or best age for learning to read

For children in standard schools, it is very important to learn to read on schedule, by the timetable dictated by the school. If you fall behind you will be unable to keep up with the rest of the curriculum and may be marked as someone who should repeat a grade, or as a person with some sort of mental handicap. In standard schools learning to read is the key to all of the rest of learning. First you "learn to read" and then you "read to learn." Without knowing how to read you can't learn much of the rest of the curriculum, because so much of it is presented through the written word. There is even evidence that failure to learn to read on schedule predicts subsequent naughtiness in standard schools. One longitudinal study (Halonen, 2006), conducted in Finland, found that poor reading in preschool and kindergarten predicted poor reading later on in elementary school and also predicted subsequent "externalizing problem behavior," which basically means acting out.

But the story is entirely different for unschooled children. They may learn to read at any time, with no apparent negative consequences. The stories sent to me by readers of this blog include 21 separate cases of children learning to read in which the age of first real reading (reading and understanding of novel passages of text) was mentioned. Of these, two learned at age 4, seven learned at age 5 or 6, six learned at age 7 or 8, five learned at age 9 or 10, and one learned at age 11.

Even within the same family, different children learned to read at quite different ages. Diane wrote that her first daughter learned to read at age 5 and her second daughter learned at age 9; Lisa W. wrote that one son learned at age 4 and another at age 7; and Beatrice wrote that one daughter learned before age 5 and the other at age 8.

None of these children has difficulty reading today. Beatrice reports that the daughter who didn't read until age 8 is now (at the time of her writing) 14 and "reads hundreds of books a year, . . . has written a novel, . . . and has won numerous poetry awards." Apparently, late reading is not inconsistent with subsequent extraordinary literary ability. This daughter did, however, show other signs of literary precocity well before she learned to read. According to Beatrice, she could recite from memory all of the poems in the *Complete Mother Goose* book by the time she was 15 months.

The message repeated most often in these stories is that, because the children were not forced or coaxed into reading against their wills, they developed positive attitudes about reading and about learning in general. This was perhaps most clearly stated by Jenny, who wrote, regarding her daughter (then age 15) who didn't read well until age 11: "One of the best things that came out of allowing her to read at her own pace and on her own initiative was that she owned the experience, and through owning that experience she came to realize that if she could do that, she could learn anything. We have never pressured her to learn anything at all, ever, and because of that, her ability to learn has remained intact. She is bright and inquisitive and interested in the world around her."

2. Motivated children can go from apparent non-reading to fluent reading very quickly
In some cases unschooled children progress from non-reading to reading in what seems to observers to be a flash. For example, Lisa W. wrote: "Our second child, who is a visual thinker, didn't learn to read until he was 7. For years, he could either figure out what he needed to know from pictorial cues, or if stuck, would get his older brother to read to him. I remember the day he started reading. He had asked his older brother to read something to him on the computer and his brother replied, 'I have better things to do than to read to you all day,' and walked away. Within days he was reading quite well."

Diane wrote, "My first daughter could not read when she

turned 5 in March but by the end of that year she could read fluently, out loud, without pause or hesitation." And Kate wrote that her son, at age 9, "taught himself to read" in a period of just one month. In that time span he deliberately worked at reading, on his own, and progressed from being a hesitant, poor reader to highly fluent reading, well beyond what a standard school would have regarded as his grade level.

Such step-like progressions in overt reading ability may occur at least partly because earlier, more covert stages of learning are not noticed by observers and may not even be noticed by the learners. Karen attributes the rapid onset of reading that she observed in her son to a sudden gain in confidence. She wrote: "Over this past summer, son A (now age 7) went from hiding his ability [to read at all] to reading chapter books. In a summer! Now, six months later, he feels confident enough in his reading ability that I regularly get up in the morning to find him reading aloud to his sister. He even offers to read to his father and me. This was unheard of a year ago when he hid his ability level from us in his embarrassment and lack of confidence. I'm so glad we didn't push him!"

3. Attempts to push reading can backfire

Three of the people who sent me stories wrote that they at some point attempted to teach reading to their non-reading child and that the attempt seemed to have negative consequences. Here is what they said.

Holli wrote that when her son was "about 3½" she began trying to teach him reading. "I think the Bob books are stupidly repetitive and inane, but I found ones that were at least moderately engaging and had him start practicing them. . . . He really was not ready yet, I think, for actual reading, and whether he was or not, he resented being made to do something that wasn't his idea, so he resisted. . . . Pretty quickly I realized that in spite of the progress he was making in reading skill, I was doing more harm than good to my son, because I was making him hate reading. I immediately ceased formal instruction in reading, and just went back to reading to him whenever he wanted me to." Holli went on to note that, roughly two years later, her son "entirely surreptitiously" began to look at books on his own and eventually to read, apparently hiding his interest and practice so as not to feel pressured.

Beatrice wrote, of her daughter who learned to read at age 8: "I too am guilty of trying to 'make her' read, when she turned 6, worried that the kids at school would be learning this skill and not wanting her to be left behind. After a couple of weeks of insisting she read and keep a journal with me spelling everything and she copying it all out, she told me flatly to 'leave me alone,' that she would have no part in my scheme and would learn to read when she was 'good and ready.'"

And Kate, a homeschooling mom in the UK, wrote, concerning her attempts to teach reading to her son: "By age 9 he was resistant to any English and reading became a regular battle. He resisted it and found it boring and he was distracted, so finally I got over my own schooly head and tried a new policy of letting go. I said that I would never make him read again or even suggest it. . . . Over the next month he quietly went to his room . . . and taught himself to read. . . . I had spent four years teaching him the basics when he wasn't interested, but am now sure that he could have learnt that in a few weeks."

4. Children learn to read when reading becomes, to them, a means to some valued end or ends

There's an old joke, which I recall first hearing several decades ago, about a child who reached age 5 without ever speaking a word. Then one day, at lunch, he said, "This soup is cold." His mom, practically falling over, said, "My son, you can talk! Why haven't you ever said anything before?" "Well," said the boy, "up until now the soup has always been warm."

This story is completely apocryphal as applied to learning to talk, which is why we understand it to be a joke. Children learn to talk whether or not they really have to talk in order to get their needs met; they are genetically programmed for it. But the story, somewhat modified, could apply quite reasonably to learning to read. Children seem to learn to read, on their own, when they see some good reason for it. Many of the stories sent to me illustrate this idea. Here are some examples:

Amanda wrote, concerning her daughter who attends a Sudbury model school: "She had consistently told people that she didn't know how to read until she made brownies this past November [at age 7]. She asked her father and myself to make her favorite brownies for her, but neither of us was willing to make them. A little while later she ran into the room and asked me if I would turn on the oven for her and find her a 9x11 pan (she said, '9 ex 11' instead of '9 by 11'). I got her a pan and turned on the oven. Later she ran in and asked me to put the brownies in the oven. Then she said, 'Ma, I think I can read now.' She brought me a few books that she then read out loud to me until she jumped up and said, 'those brownies smell done. Will you take them out now?' . . . Now she tells people that she knows how to read and that she taught herself how."

Idzie, a 19-year-old (at the time) unschooled but beautifully educated blogger, sent me a link to an essay, on her blog, about her own memories of learning to read. She wrote, in part: "When I was something like age 8 or 9, my mother was reading the first Harry Potter book aloud to my sister and me. But, well, she had things to do other than read, and if she read too long, her voice would get hoarse. So, being quite frustrated at how slow a process this was, and really wanting to know what happened next, I picked it up and began to read."

Marie, an unschooling mom, wrote about her son, now age 7: "[He] found the incentive to become a better reader through acting at a local theater. He has always been passionate about putting together 'shows,' but now he is old enough to have real acting experience. He sees that reading is an integral part of this activity that he loves and it has given him a strong reason to grow and develop as a reader. He recently had a part in *A Midsummer Night's Dream* and had to read and memorize Shakespeare. It took no instruction on the part of a 'teacher' whatsoever."

Jenny wrote that her daughter, who didn't begin to read books until age 11, was able to satisfy her love of stories by being read to, watching movies, and checking out CDs and books on tape from the library. She finally began reading because there was no other way for her to satisfy her interest in video games, such as ToonTown, and manga books, which require reading that nobody would do for her.

5. Reading, like many other skills, is learned socially through shared participation

Observations at Sudbury Valley School, and at other Sudbury model schools, suggest that many children there learn to read through age-mixed play. Non-readers and readers play games together, including computer games, with written words. To keep the game going, the readers read the words and the non-readers pick them up.

Vincent Lopez, a staff member at the Diablo Valley School, a Sudbury model school, sent me this sweet example of age-mixed learning: "In the art room they are making signs to imitate a TV show that had just started. It is in my opinion, a dumb, low-ethics, media-driven, free for all dating show; I've let this be known before. In their own way they are processing the future to come. . . . but I digress. The jewel of this snippet is that the 5-year-old is attempting to read the sign with the help of his multi-aged peers. . . . Students learn because they want to get the jokes, be more advanced like the peers around them."

Nearly all of the stories from home unschoolers include examples of shared participation in reading. One of my favorites is that presented by Diane, who noted that her daughter, who learned to read at age 5, became interested in reading because of the family's regular Bible reading time. Before she could read she insisted on having her turn at Bible reading, "and she would just make up words as her turn!"

Others wrote about shared family games involving words, or about shared television viewing in which the onscreen guide and captions would be read for the benefit of nonreaders. Over time, the nonreaders needed ever less help; they began recognizing and reading more and more words themselves. The most often mentioned examples of shared participation are those of parents, or sometimes siblings, reading stories to nonreaders, often as part of a bedtime ritual. Nonreaders look on, at the words as well as the pictures, and sometimes read some of the words; or they memorize books that have been read to them repeatedly, and then later they pretend to read the books while actually attending to some of the words. Pretend reading gradually becomes real reading.

Decades ago the Russian developmental psychologist Lev Vygotsky expounded on the theory that children acquire new skills first socially, through joint participation with more skilled others, and then later begin to use the new skills privately, for their own purposes. That general principle certainly seems to hold in the case of reading.

6. Some children become interested in writing before reading, and they learn to read as they learn to write

At least seven of the people who sent me stories said that their child was interested in writing, or typing, either before or simultaneously with their initial interest in reading. Here are four examples:

Marie wrote, of her son, now age 7: "He is an artist and

spends hours drawing things, especially stories and inventions. So naturally he wished to make his pictures 'talk' with captions, titles, instructions, and quotations. . . . There was a lot of 'MOM? How do you spell Superdog wants to go home?' I would spell out the sentence and five minutes later, 'MOM? How do you spell Superdog sees his house?' This boy learned to read, at least in part, by reading the sentences that he, himself, had written.

Beatrice told a similar story about her youngest daughter, who learned to read before age 5. "She learned to read from her desire to express herself through the written word. Starting from the time she could hold a pencil, be it writing a poem, a song, designing an ad, she needed me to tell her the spelling: 'How do you spell beaver, how do you spell suggest?'"

Lisa R. wrote of her son, who was in the midst of learning to read: "His reading skill relates to his writing efforts. . . . He has written short notes and story titles using his own phonetic spelling. Sometimes he asks how to spell words for a note or a book. Through repetition, he now remembers some of these words."

Lisa W. wrote: "Our oldest child learned to read when he was 4 years old as a by-product of trying to find free online games on the computer. He would open the browser and ask me to spell free, then online, then games. All of a sudden he was reading."

7. There is no predictable "course" through which children learn to read

Lest you leave this essay with the belief that I and the people who have contributed these stories have taught you something useful about how to "teach" or "help" your child to read, I assure you we have not. Every child is unique. Your child must tell you how you can help, or not help. I have no idea about that, nor does any so-called reading expert. My only advice is, don't push it; listen to your child; respond appropriately to your child's questions, but don't go overboard by telling your child more than he or she wants to know. If you do go overboard, your child may learn to stop asking you questions.

Quite a few of the people who wrote to me expressed surprise at the sequence that their child went through in learning to read. Some learned to read big and exotic words, like *hippopotamus* or *Tyrannosaurus*, which never appear in the primers, well before they learned simpler words. Some, as I said, learned to write before they could read. Some seemed to be learning at a rapid rate and then they just stopped for a couple of years before progressing further. We adults can enjoy watching all of this as long as we remember that it isn't our responsibility to change it. We're just observers and sometimes tools that our children use for their own chosen ends.

I am very grateful to the people who took time to write their stories so thoughtfully and send them to me. Since this study was conducted I have received quite a few more such stories, which, collectively, add further confirmation to what I have written here. Finally, I can't resist ending this essay with a little story about my son's learning to read. He was a very early reader, and one of the first indications of his reading ability occurred when he was about 3½ and we were looking at a Civil War monument in a town square somewhere in New England. He looked at the words, and then he said to me, "Why would men fight and die to save an onion?" He clearly had read the word "union" phonetically and was quite appropriately mystified.

References

Gray (2008). Children educate themselves IV: Lessons from Sudbury Valley. Available at https://www.psychologytoday.com/us/blog/freedom-learn/200808/children-educate-themselves-iv-lessons-sudbury-valley.

Halonen, A., et al. (2006). The role of learning to read in the development of problem behaviour: A cross-lagged longitudinal study. *British Journal of Educational Psychology*, 76, 517-534.

Rose, D., & Dalton, B. (2009). Learning to read in the digital age. *Mind, Brain, and Education*, 3, 74-83.

2

The Reading Wars

Why Natural Learning Fails in Classrooms

The best practices for teaching reading in school do not mimic natural learning

NOVEMBER 19, 2013

Progressive educators have always believed that methods of classroom instruction should be based on children's natural ways of learning; that is, on the ways that children learn in life outside of classrooms. This has led to a variety of meaning-centered ways of teaching, which run counter to what we might call the process-centered ways of so-called traditional education or direct instruction.

For example, in teaching arithmetic, the progressive educator might set up conditions aimed at helping children discover, or at least understand, the purpose and meaning of multiplication. In contrast, the traditionalist might drill children on the multiplication tables and later teach a step-by-step algorithm for multiplying two-digit numbers, with little or no attention to the question of why anyone would be interested in multiplication or why the algorithm works.

In teaching reading, the progressive educator might focus on ways to help beginners recognize and thereby read whole words from the outset and allow them to figure out or guess at other words from the context (such as from pictures and the meaning of adjacent words), so they are reading for meaning right from the beginning. In contrast, the traditionalist might start with lessons on letter recognition and the relation of letters to sounds (phonics) before moving on to whole words and sentences. The process of reading requires the decoding of letters into sounds, and the traditionalist teaches this process explicitly before becoming concerned with meaning.

This essay is about the teaching and learning of reading. I'm going to argue that the ways that children learn to read naturally, in life outside of the classroom, fail when they are imported into the classroom. Let's start with children who teach themselves to read outside of school.

Precocious Readers

Roughly five percent of children enter first grade already knowing how to read reasonably well, and perhaps as many as one percent, referred to as precocious readers, read fluently by age 4 (Olson et al., 2006). I have witnessed this phenomenon twice, as my youngest brother and my son were both precocious readers. I have no idea how they learned, but I can assure you that nobody deliberately taught them. They were read to a lot, they were surrounded by reading materials and by people who read, and they somehow just picked it up.

Researchers have conducted systematic case studies of precocious readers, through interviews of parents, and have compared them with other children to see if they are unique in any ways other than their early reading. The results of such studies, overall, support the following conclusions (Margrain, 2005; Olson et al., 2006):

- Precocious reading does not depend on unusually high IQ or any particular personality trait. Although some precocious readers have IQ scores in the gifted range, many others score about average. Personality tests likewise reveal no consistent differences between precocious readers and other children.

- Precocious reading is not strongly linked to social class. Some studies have found it to be as frequent in blue-collar as in white-collar families. However, it does seem to depend on growing up in a family where reading is a common and valued activity.

- Parents of precocious readers report that they or an older sibling of the child often read to the child, but did not in any systematic way attempt to teach reading. In the typical case, the parents at some point discovered, to their surprise, that their child was reading, at least in a preliminary way, and then they fostered that reading by providing appropriate reading materials, answering the child's questions about words, and in some cases pointing out the

relationship between letters and sounds to help with un-
familiar words. In essentially no cases, however, did they
provide anything like the systematic training in either
phonics or word recognition that might occur in school.

In sum, precocious readers appear to be children who
grow up in a literate home and, for some unknown reason
(unlike even their siblings in the same home), develop an intense early interest in reading. Interest, not unusual brain development, is what distinguishes them from others. Because
they are interested and strongly motivated, they use whatever
cues are available to figure out the meanings of printed words
and sentences, and, along the way, with or without help, con-
sciously or unconsciously, they eventually infer the underlying phonetic code and use it to read new words. For them,
reading for meaning comes first, before phonics. In the words
of one set of researchers (Olson et al, 2006), "[The precocious
readers] were not taught the prerequisite skills of reading
such as phoneme-grapheme correspondence or letter-naming
skills but, instead, learned to read familiar, meaningful sight
vocabulary; the rules of reading were not explicitly taught but
apparently inferred over time."

The fact that precocious readers learn to read relatively
quickly, before they are 4 years old, with no evidence of stress
and much evidence of pleasure, suggests that learning to read
in this way is not very difficult when a person really wants to
do it. Learning to read, for them, quite literally, is child's play.

How Unschoolers and Children in
Democratic Schools Learn to Read

In the first essay in this collection, I presented a qualitative analysis of case histories of learning to read by children in unschooling families (who don't send their children to school or teach a curriculum at home) and by children at the Sudbury Valley School (where students are in charge of their own education and there is no imposed curriculum or instruction). I won't repeat that work in detail here, but, in brief, some of the main conclusions were these: (1) Children in these settings learn to read at a wide variety of ages; (2) at whatever age they learn, they learn quite quickly when they are truly motivated to do so; (3) attempts by parents to teach reading to unmotivated children generally fail and often seem to delay the child's interest in reading; and (4) being read to and engaging in meaningful ways with literary material with skilled readers (older children or adults) facilitates learning.

In sum, these children seem to learn to read in essentially the same ways that precocious readers learn, but at a wide variety of ages. They learn when and because they are interested in reading, and they use whatever information is available to help them, including information provided by people who already know how to read. They are not systematically taught, and the people who help them generally have no training or expertise in the teaching of reading.

The Reading Wars: The Debate about
How to Teach Reading in Schools

We turn now from self-motivated, self-directed children learning to read out of school to children who are taught in school, where the assumption is that they must learn to read at a certain age and in a certain way, whether they want to or not. In school, learning to read appears to be unnatural and difficult. It occurs at a snail's pace, incrementally over several years. Even after three or four years of training many children are not fluent readers.

Progressive educators have always believed that learning to read should not be slow and tedious. They have argued for "whole-word" and "whole-language" methods of teaching reading, which, they claim, are more natural and pleasurable than phonics-first methods. Although progressive educators commonly think of themselves as proposing something new, contrasted with "traditional education," the progressive arguments actually go back at least to the origin of compulsory state schooling in America. Horace Mann, the first secretary of education in any state in the union, who oversaw the passage of the first state compulsory education law (in Massachusetts, in 1852), fought for the whole-word approach and railed against phonics. Likewise, in the early 20th century John Dewey and progressive educators inspired by him were champions of holistic, reading-for-meaning methods. Later, in the 1970s and '80s, Kenneth Goodman and Frank Smith took up the torch and promoted what they called the whole-language approach.

On the other side are those who have long argued that

phonics is the key to reading and should be taught early and directly. Noah Webster, sometimes referred to as the father of American scholarship and education, was an early warrior in the phonics camp. In the late 18th century, he created the first series of books designed to teach reading and spelling in secular schools, and they were founded on phonics. In the mid 20th century, Rudolph Flesch turned the tide back toward phonics, away from progressive methods promoted by Dewey and others, with his bestselling book, *Why Johnny Can't Read* (1955). He argued convincingly that the progressive movement had produced a serious decline in reading ability in American schoolchildren because it ignored phonics. In the most recent two decades, the leading proponents of phonics include educational researchers who base their argument on research and data more than theory. Many carefully controlled experiments have by now been conducted to compare the reading scores of children taught by different methods in different classrooms, and the results of the great majority of them favor phonics (Kim, 2008).

Because of their intensity and presumed importance, these debates about how to teach reading have long been dubbed "the Reading Wars." Today, the majority (though not all) of the experts who have examined the data have declared that the wars are over—phonics has won. The data seem clear. Overall, schoolchildren who are taught phonics from the beginning become better readers, sooner, than those who are taught by whole-word or whole-language methods. The learning is still slow and tedious, but not as slow and tedious for phonics learners as for those taught by other methods.

Why Natural Learning Fails in Classrooms

So, we have this puzzle. Out of school, children learn to read by what appear to be whole-word, whole-language methods. They read right off for meaning and they learn to recognize words and read whole passages before they pay much attention to individual letters or sounds. Phonics comes later, based on inferences that may be conscious or unconscious. Learning to read out of school is in some ways like learning oral language; you learn it, including the rules, with little awareness that you are learning it and little awareness of the rules that underlie it. But that doesn't work well for learning to read in school. Learning there is better if you master the rules (the rules relating letters to sounds) before attending much to meaning.

The mistake of the progressive educators, I think, has been to assume that the classroom is or can be a natural learning environment. It isn't, and for the most part it can't be. The classroom is a setting where you have a rather large group of children, all about the same age, and a teacher whose primary tasks are to keep order and impart a curriculum—the same curriculum for everyone. In that setting, the teacher decides what to do; not the students. If students decided, they would all decide on different things and there would be chaos. No matter how liberal-minded the teacher is, real, prolonged self-direction and self-motivation is not possible in the classroom. In this setting, children must suppress their own interests, not follow them. While children out of school learn what and because they want to, children in school must learn, or at least go through the motions of learning, what the teacher wants them to learn in the way the teacher wants them to do it. The result is slow, tedious, shallow learning that is about procedure, not meaning, regardless of the teacher's intent.

The classroom is all about training. Training is the process of getting reluctant organisms to do or learn what the trainer wants them to do or learn. Under those conditions, methods that focus on the mechanical processes underlying reading—the conversion of sights to sounds—work better than methods that attempt to promote reading through meaning, which requires that students care about the meaning, which requires that they be able to follow their own interests, which is not possible in the classroom.

It happens, by coincidence perhaps, that my brothers' and my experiences of learning to read, decades ago, nicely illustrate the story I have described here. I was taught reading by the "look and say" whole-word method (with Dick and Jane books), and I couldn't read fluently until about fourth grade. My somewhat younger brother was taught from first grade on by a method strongly focused on phonics, and he could read fluently by second grade. My youngest brother taught himself to read at home, with no explicit instruction, and could read fluently before he was 4 years old.

References

Kim, J. S. (2008). Research and the reading wars. In: Hess, F. M. (Ed.), *When research matters: How scholarship influences education policy*, 89-111. Cambridge, MA: Harvard Education Press.

Margrain, V. G. (2005). Precocious readers: Case studies of
    spontaneous learning, self-regulation and social support in the
    early years. Doctoral Dissertation, Victoria University of
    Wellington, School of Education. New Zealand.

Olson, L. A., Evans, J. R., & Keckler, W. T. (2006). Precocious
    readers: Past, present, and future. *Journal for the Education of
    the Gifted*, 30, 205-235.

3

Differences Between Self-Directed and Progressive Education

Self-Directed Education, not progressive education, is the wave of the future

JUNE 27, 2017

As you may know, I'm an advocate for Self-Directed Education. My research and that of others convinces me that Self-Directed Education works, is eminently practical, and is far less trouble to everyone involved than the coercive educational system that we all consider to be standard schooling. Self-Directed Education, with capital letters, is the term that is increasingly being used for the educational practice of people who call themselves "unschoolers" or who attend schools or learning centers specifically designed to support self-direction, with no imposed curriculum, such as Sudbury model democratic schools, Agile Learning Centers, and some schools that call themselves "free schools" (Gray, 2017).

I've found that when I speak or write about Self-Directed

Education some people mistakenly believe that I'm speaking or writing about progressive education. Progressive education has many of the same goals as Self-Directed Education, and its advocates use much of the same language, but the foundational philosophy is quite different and the methodology is very different. In what follows I'll review the basic tenets of progressive education, then review those of Self-Directed Education, and, finally, explain why I think the latter, not the former, will become the standard mode of education in the not-too-distant future.

Progressive Education

Progressive education is the term generally applied to an educational reform movement that began in the late 19th century, around the same time that schooling became compulsory in most U.S. states, and has waxed and waned at least twice since then. The period from about 1890 to about 1940 saw a flowering of progressive ideas in education, the birth of many progressive private schools, and some concerted efforts to bring progressive ideas into mainstream public schools. The leading philosopher of progressive education at that time, at least in the United States, was John Dewey. Other early progressive thinkers in education included Rudolf Steiner (1869-1925) and Maria Montessori (1870-1952), whose traditions live on, respectively, in Waldorf and Montessori schools. Progressive ideas in education tended to fade with World War II and its aftermath, tended to bloom again in the 1960s and '70s, and have generally been declining ever since about 1980. There is, however, some recent revival of progressive education in schools that emphasize project-based learning.

Progressive educators typically emphasize learning by doing, contextual learning relevant to students' real life experiences, critical thinking, deep understanding rather than rote memory, group work and collaboration rather than competitions, evaluation based on products rather than tests, and the fostering of social responsibility, democratic attitudes, and concern for social justice. They commonly talk about "educating the whole person" and about "student focused" as opposed to simply subject-focused education. Progressive teachers are expected to get to know all of their students as individuals and bring out the best in each of them.

A good description of progressive education can be found on the website of the Progressive Education Network (a nonprofit organization formed in 2009 as part of an attempt to revive progressive education). The website states:

> "Education must (a) amplify students' voice, agency, conscience, and intellect to create a more equitable, just, and sustainable world; (b) encourage the active participation of students in their learning, in their communities, and in the world; (c) respond to the developmental needs of students, and focus on their social, emotional, intellectual, cognitive, cultural, and physical development; (d) honor and nurture students' natural curiosity and innate desire to learn, fostering internal motivation, and the discovery of passion and purpose; (e) emerge from the interests, experiences, goals, and needs of diverse constituents, fos-

tering empathy, communication and collaboration across difference: and (f) foster respectfully collaborative and critical relationships between students, educators, parents/guardians, and the community."

Alfie Kohn (2008), one of today's leading advocates for progressive education, has argued that schools can be rated as more or less progressive to the degree that they are committed to (a) attending to the whole child, not just to academics; (b) community; (c) collaboration; (d) social justice; (e) fostering intrinsic motivation; (f) deep understanding; (g) active learning; and (h) taking kids seriously.

Progressive educators tend to view education as a collaborative endeavor between students and their teacher. A good deal of initiative comes from the students, but the teacher is responsible to guide that initiative in productive ways. The child's intrinsic interests play a large role, but the teacher "nurtures" or even "brings out" those interests in the child. Play is understood to be part of the learning process, but the teacher guides and interprets that play in ways designed to ensure certain educative ends.

Self-Directed Education

Advocates of Self-Directed Education, like those of progressive education, emphasize that education is about much more than academic learning. The website of the Alliance for Self-Directed Education defines education as "the sum of everything a person learns that enables that person to live a satisfying and meaningful life." That would include knowledge of oneself, skills in planning and directing one's own activities, skills in how to get along well with other people, and an understanding of the world around oneself sufficient to navigate that world effectively. Most progressive educators would agree, I think, with this kind of definition of education.

The difference between progressive education and Self-Directed Education lies in the understanding of how such whole-person education occurs. To the progressive educator it emerges from a collaboration between the child and a benevolent, extraordinarily competent teacher, who gently guides the child's energy and shapes the child's raw ideas in ways that serve the child's and society's long-term good. To the advocate of Self-Directed Education it emerges out of children's natural drives to understand themselves and the world around them and to use whatever resources are available in their environment, including knowledgeable and skilled others, to achieve that end.

To advocates of Self-Directed Education, it is the child's brilliance, not a teacher's, that enables education. The job of adults who facilitate Self-Directed Education is less onerous than that of teachers in progressive education. In Self-Directed Education adults do not need to have great knowledge of every subject a student might want to learn, do not have to understand the workings of every child's mind, and do not have to be masters of pedagogy (whatever on earth that might be). Rather, they simply (though this is not always simple) have to be sure that the child is provided with an environment that allows the child's natural educative instincts to operate effectively.

As I have argued elsewhere (e.g. Gray, 2016), the ideal environment for Self-Directed Education is one in which the child (a) has unlimited time and freedom to play and explore; (b) has access to the most useful tools of the culture; (c) is embedded in a caring community of people who range widely in age and exemplify a wide variety of skills, knowledge, and ideas; and (d) has access to a number of adults who are willing to answer questions (or try to answer them) and provide help when asked. This is the kind of environment that is established at schools or learning centers designed for Self-Directed Education, and it is also the kind of environment that successful unschooling families provide for their children.

Education, in this view, is not a collaboration of student and a teacher; it is entirely the job of the student. While progressive educators continue to see it as their responsibility to ensure that students acquire certain knowledge, skills, and values, and to evaluate students' progress, facilitators of Self-Directed Education do not see that as their responsibility. While progressive education is on a continuum with traditional education, Self-Directed Education represents a complete break from traditional education.

I wish here to introduce a distinction (also presented on the website of the Alliance for Self-Directed Education) between Self-Directed Education (or SDE), with capital letters, and self-directed education (or sde), with small letters. The former (with capital letters), as I noted at the outset of this essay, refers to the education of children, of K-12 school age, whose families have made a deliberate decision that the children will educate themselves by following their own interests, without an imposed curriculum. In contrast, the latter (sde) is used as a more generic term to refer to something that every human being is engaged in essentially every waking minute of every day. We are all, constantly, educating ourselves as we pursue our interests, make our living, and strive to solve problems in our daily lives. Most of what any of us know— regardless of how much curriculum-based schooling we have attended—has come from self-directed education.

Those who advocate for Self-Directed Education (capital letters) are, in effect, saying that self-directed education (small letters) is so powerful and effective that children don't need imposed education at all, if they are provided with an environment that optimizes their ability to educate themselves. In fact, many are saying, as do I, that imposed education interferes with self-directed education by consuming so much of children's time, turning learning into something unpleasant, and planting in children's minds the idea that they are not capable of controlling their own education.

Why I Think Self-Directed Education, Not Progressive Education, Will Become the Standard Mode of Future Education

I admire progressive educators. Without exception, those I have met are good people, who care deeply about children and want to make children's lives better. They see the harm of our standard system of education and want to do something about it. Progressive educators are at the forefront, right now, of attempts to reduce homework (so children will have a life outside of school), bring back recess, reduce or eliminate standardized testing, and allow teachers to be more flexible and responsive to children's needs in the classroom. They are fighting an uphill battle, and I admire them for it. But this is a battle that has been going on for as long as we have had compulsory schooling. It is a battle that helps to modulate the excesses of standard education; but it is incapable of defeating it, because it accepts too much of the standard set of beliefs about what education must be.

As long as teachers believe that it is their task to make sure that children learn certain things, at certain times in their development, then no matter how progressive their thinking, they will have to use coercive methods to get children to do that. Children do not, by nature, all develop similar interests at the same time, so it is impossible to operate in anything like a typical classroom, with more than a handful of students, on the assumption that all students will learn the expected curriculum by doing what interests them.

I dare say that most new teachers, emerging from schools of education, enter their job thinking they are going to be progressive educators. They went into teaching, after all, because they love children; and in their education classes much if not most of the educational philosophy they read and heard about was progressive philosophy—about guiding, nurturing, and enabling, not about coercing. But then they entered the real world of the classroom. There they had 30 children, and had to keep order, and had to do something to make it seem like learning was going on; and their progressive ideas soon flew out the window. It's no surprise that those schools that do operate in most accord with progressive principles are private and very expensive. They require small classes, a high ratio of teachers to students, and extraordinarily competent, dedicated teachers.

Even ardent advocates of progressive education admit that one of the reasons progressive education has not taken off is that it is so demanding of teachers. Here, for example, is what Alfie Kohn (2008) has to say about that: "It [progressive education] is much more demanding [than traditional education] of teachers, who have to know their subject matter inside and out if they want their students to make sense of biology or literature as opposed to simply memorizing the frog's anatomy or the sentence's structure. But progressive teachers also have to know a lot about pedagogy because no amount of content knowledge (say, expertise in science or English) can tell you how to facilitate learning." Add to that the idea that teachers are supposed to get to know all of their students as individuals and help them develop their full potential and their own interests, and you can perhaps begin to understand why progressive education has not replaced direct, drill-and-test education as the standard method.

Progressive educators often cite Jean-Jacques Rousseau as an early proponent of their views. Rousseau's sole work on education was his book *Émile*, first published in 1760, which is a fictional account of the education of a single boy. If this book has any real-world application at all it would be to the education of a prince. Émile's teacher is a tutor, whose sole job, sole mission in life, is the education of this one boy, a teacher-student ratio of one to one. The tutor, by Rousseau's description, is a sort of superhero. He is not only extraordinarily knowledgeable in all subjects, but he understands Émile inside and out, more so than it is ever possible (I would say) for any actual human being to understand another human being. He knows all of the boy's desires, at any given time, and he knows exactly what stimuli to provide at any time to maximize the educational benefits that will accrue from the boy's acting on those desires. Thus, the tutor creates an environment in which Émile is always doing just what he wants to do, yet is learning precisely the lessons that the tutor has masterfully laid out for him.

I think if more educators actually read Émile, rather than just referred to the book, they would recognize the basic flaw in progressive educational theory. It is way too demanding of teachers to be practical on any sort of mass scale, and it makes unrealistic assumptions about the predictability and visibility of human desires and motives. (For more on my analysis of *Émile*, see Gray, 2015.) At best, on a mass scale, progressive educational philosophy can simply help to modulate the harshness of traditional methods and add a bit of self-direction and creativity to students' lives in school.

In contrast to progressive education, Self-Directed Education is inexpensive and efficient. The Sudbury Valley School, for example, operates on a per-student budget less than half that of the local public schools. A large ratio of adults to students is not needed, because most student learning does not come from interaction with adults. In this age-mixed setting, younger students are continuously learning from older ones, and children of all ages practice essential skills and try out ideas in their play, exploration, conversations, and pursuits of whatever interests they develop. They also, on their own initiative, use books and, in today's world, Internet resources to acquire the knowledge they are seeking at any given time.

The usual criticism of Self-Directed Education is that it can't work, or can work only for certain, highly self-motivated people. In fact, progressive educators are often quick to draw a distinction between their view of education and that of Self-Directed Education, because they don't want their view to be confused with ideas that they consider to be "romantic" or "crazy" and unworkable. For example, I'm pretty sure that Alfie Kohn (2008) had Self-Directed Education in mind when he wrote: "In this cartoon version of the tradition, kids are free to do anything they please, the curriculum can consist of whatever is fun (and nothing that isn't fun). Learning is thought to happen automatically while the teachers just stand by, observing and beaming. I lack the space here to offer examples of this sort of misrepresentation—or a full account of why it's so profoundly wrong—but trust me: People really do sneer at the idea of progressive education based on an image that has little to do with progressive education."

Kohn's "cartoon" characterization of Self-Directed Education is not quite right—because children do, on their own, regularly choose to do things that aren't fun in an immediate sense and because staff members don't just stand around observing and beaming; but, yet, it is not too far off the mark.

And it does work. Don't trust me on that; read and think skeptically about the evidence. Follow-up studies of graduates of schools for Self-Directed Education and of grown unschoolers have shown that people, who educated themselves by following their own interests, are doing very well in life (for a summary of such studies and references, see Gray, 2017).

Self-Directed Education works because we are biologically designed for it. Throughout essentially all of human history, children educated themselves by exploring, playing, watching and listening to others, and figuring out and pursuing their own goals in life (Gray, 2016). In an extensive review of the anthropological literature on education cross-culturally, David Lancy (2016) concluded that learning—including the learning that comprises education—is natural to human beings, but teaching and being taught is not. Winston Churchill's claim, "I always like to learn, but I don't always like to be taught," is something that anyone, any time, any place, could have said.

Children's educative instincts still work beautifully, in our modern society, as long as we provide the conditions that enable them to work. The same instincts that motivated hunter-gatherer children to learn to hunt, gather, and do all that they had to do to become effective adults motivate children to learn to read, calculate with numbers, operate computers, and do all that they have to do to become effective adults in our society today (Gray, 2016). Self-Directed Education is so natural, so much more pleasant and efficient for everyone than is coercive education, that it seems inevitable to me that it will once again become the standard educational route.

Coercive schooling has been a blip in human history, designed to serve temporary ends that arose with industrialization and the need to suppress creativity and free will (Gray, 2008). Coercive schooling is in the process now of burning itself out, in a kind of final flaring up. Once people rediscover that Self-Directed Education works, and doesn't cause the stress and harm that coercive schooling does, and we begin to divert some fraction of the billions of dollars currently spent on coercive education to the provision of resources for Self-Directed Education for all children, Self-Directed Education will once again become the standard educational route. Then we'll be able to drop the capital letters. And then we won't need progressive education to soften the harsh blows of coercive education.

References

Gray, P. (2008). A brief history of education. In P. Gray Freedom to learn blog, *Psychology Today*. Online at https://www.psychologytoday.com/us/blog/freedom-learn/200808/brief-history-education.

Gray, P. (2015). Rousseau's errors: They persist today in educational theory. *Issues in Early Education*, 3, 23-28.

Gray, P. (2016). Children's natural ways of learning still work—even for the three Rs. In D. C. Geary & D. B. Berch (eds), *Evolutionary perspectives on child development and education* (pp 33-66). Springer.

Gray, P. (2017). Self-directed education—unschooling and democratic schooling. In G. Noblit (Ed.), *Oxford research encyclopedia of education*. New York: Oxford University Press.

Kohn, A. (2008). Progressive education: Why it's hard to beat but also hard to find. Independent School, Spring. Online at https://www.alfiekohn.org/article/progressive-education/

Lancy, D. (2016). Teaching: natural or cultural? In D. C. Geary & D. B. Berch (eds), *Evolutionary perspectives on child development and education* (pp 67-93). Springer.

4

When Less Is More

The Case for Teaching Less Math in School

*In an experiment, children who
were taught less learned more*

MARCH 18, 2010

In 1929, the superintendent of schools in Ithaca, New York, sent out a challenge to his colleagues in other cities. "What," he asked, "can we drop from the elementary school curriculum?" He complained that over the years new subjects were continuously being added and nothing was being subtracted, with the result that the school day was packed with too many subjects and there was little time to reflect seriously on anything. This was back in the days when people believed that children shouldn't have to spend all of their time at school work—that they needed some time to play, to do chores at home, and to be with their families—so there was reason back then to believe that whenever something new is added to the curriculum something else should be dropped.

One of the recipients of this challenge was L. P. Benezet (1935/1936), superintendent of schools in Manchester, New Hampshire, who responded with this outrageous proposal: We should drop arithmetic! Benezet went on to argue that the time spent on arithmetic in the early grades was wasted effort, or worse. In fact, he wrote: "For some years I had noted that the effect of the early introduction of arithmetic had been to dull and almost chloroform the child's reasoning facilities." All that drill, he claimed, had divorced the whole realm of numbers and arithmetic, in the children's minds, from common sense, with the result that they could do the calculations as taught to them, but didn't understand what they were doing and couldn't apply the calculations to real life problems. He believed that if arithmetic were not taught until later on—preferably not until seventh grade—the kids would learn it with far less effort and greater understanding.

Think of it. Today whenever we hear that children aren't learning much of what is taught in school the hue and cry from the educational establishment is that we must therefore teach more of it! If 200 hours of instruction on subject X does no good, well, let's try 400 hours. If children aren't learning what is taught to them in first grade, then let's start teaching it in kindergarten. And if they aren't learning it in kindergarten, that could only mean that we need to start them in pre-kindergarten! But Benezet had the opposite opinion. If kids aren't learning much math in the early grades despite considerable time and effort devoted to it, then why waste time and effort on it?

Benezet followed his outrageous suggestion with an outrageous experiment. He asked the principals and teachers in some of the schools located in the poorest parts of Manchester to drop the third R from the early grades. They would not teach arithmetic—no adding, subtracting, multiplying, or dividing. He chose schools in the poorest neighborhoods because he knew that if he tried this in the wealthier neighborhoods, where parents were high school or college graduates, the parents would rebel. As a compromise, to appease the principals who were not willing to go as far as he wished, Benezet decided on a plan in which arithmetic would be introduced in sixth grade.

As part of the plan, he asked the teachers of the earlier grades to devote some of the time that they would normally spend on arithmetic to a new third R—recitation. By "recitation" he meant, "speaking the English language." He did "not mean giving back, verbatim, the words of the teacher or the textbook" (Benezet, 1935/1936). The children would be asked to talk about topics that interested them—experiences they had had, movies they had seen, or anything that would lead to genuine, lively communication and discussion. This, he thought, would improve their abilities to reason and communicate logically. He also asked the teachers to give their pupils some practice in measuring and counting things, to assure that they would have some practical experience with numbers.

In order to evaluate the experiment, Benezet arranged for a graduate student from Boston University to come up and test the Manchester children at various times in the sixth grade. The results were remarkable. At the beginning of their sixth grade year, the children in the experimental classes, who had not been taught any arithmetic, performed much better than those in the traditional classes on story problems that could be solved by common sense and a general understanding of numbers and measurement. Of course, at the beginning of sixth grade, those in the experimental classes performed worse on the standard school arithmetic tests, where the problems were set up in the usual school manner and could be solved simply by applying the rote-learned algorithms. But by the end of sixth grade those in the experimental classes had completely caught up on this and were still way ahead of the others on story problems.

In sum, Benezet showed that kids who received just one year of arithmetic, in sixth grade, performed at least as well on standard calculations and much better on story problems. than kids who had received several previous years of arithmetic training. This was all the more remarkable because of the fact that those who received just one year of training were from the poorest neighborhoods—the neighborhoods that had previously produced the poorest test results. Why have almost no educators heard of this experiment? Why isn't Benezet now considered to be one of the geniuses of public education? I wonder.

For decades since Benezet's time, educators have debated about the best ways to teach mathematics in schools. There was the new math, the new new math, and so on. Nothing has worked. There are many reasons for this, one of which is that the people who teach in elementary schools are not mathematicians. Most of them are math phobic, just like most people in the larger culture. They, after all, are themselves products of the school system, and one thing the school system does well is to generate a lasting fear and loathing of mathematics in most people who pass through it. No matter what textbooks or worksheets or lesson plans the higher-ups devise for them, the teachers teach math by rote, in the only way they can, and they just pray that no smart-aleck student asks them a question such as "Why do we do it that way?" or "What good is this?" The students, of course, pick up on their teachers' fear, and they learn not to ask or even to think about such questions. They learn to be dumb. They learn, as Benezet would have put it, that a math-schooled mind is a chloroformed mind.

In an article published several years ago, Patricia Kenschaft, a professor of mathematics at Montclair State University, described her experiences visiting elementary schools and talking with teachers about math. In one visit to a K-6 school in New Jersey she discovered that not a single teacher, out of the 50 that she met with, knew how to find the area of a rectangle (Kenschaft, 2005). They taught multiplication, but none of them knew that multiplication is used to find the area of a rectangle. Their most common guess was that you add the length and the width to get the area. Their excuse for not knowing was that they did not need to teach about areas of rectangles; that came later in the curriculum. But the fact that they couldn't figure out that multiplication is used to find the area was evidence to Kenschaft that they didn't really know what multiplication is or what it is for. She also found that although the teachers knew and taught the algorithm for multiplying one two-digit number by another, none of them could explain why that algorithm works.

The school that Kenschaft visited happened to be in a very poor district, with mostly African American kids, so at first she figured that the worst teachers must have been assigned to that school, and she theorized that this was why African Americans do even more poorly than white Americans on math tests. But then she went into some schools in wealthy districts, with mostly white kids, and found that the mathematics knowledge of teachers there was equally pathetic. She concluded that nobody could be learning much math in school and, "It appears that the higher scores of the affluent districts are not due to superior teaching but to the supplementary informal 'home schooling' of children."

At the present time it seems clear that we are doing more damage than good by teaching math in elementary schools. Therefore, I'm with Benezet. We should stop teaching it. The same can be said of everything else taught in school, though the evidence is not quite as clear and dramatic. When children learn in their own ways, at their own schedule, in relation to their real interests, the learning is meaningful and grounded in understanding, not rote memory grounded in fear.

References

Benezet, L. P. (1935/1936). The teaching of Arithmetic: The Story of an experiment. *Journal of the National Education Association*, in three parts. Vol. 24(8), 241-244; Vol. 24(9), 301-303; & Vol. 25(1), 7-8. Also available online at http://www.inference.org. uk/sanjoy/benezet/1.html

Kenschaft, P. C. (2005). Racial equality requires teaching elementary school teachers more mathematics. *Notices of the AMS*, 52, 208-212.

5

Kids Learn Math Easily When They Control Their Own Learning

Math outside of school is fun, useful, and joyfully learned

APRIL 15, 2010

We fear it and loathe it; we admire but are also suspicious of those who are good at it; we place it in such high esteem that we make children study (or pretend to study) it almost every day of every year that they are in school; and we use it as a major criterion for college entry. We put math on a pedestal and then we avert our eyes, or else we spit at it—as happens with most things that we put on pedestals.

Math is that school subject that we can't BS our way through. That's one thing that makes it so scary to so many. There are right and wrong answers to every question, no partial credit. It also seems to many people that math performance reflects basic intelligence. To do badly is to come across as logically inept, so fear of failure is even greater in math than in other school subjects, and fear of failure always inhibits learning. I suppose the reason math counts so much on the SAT and ACT college admissions tests is that people think it is an index of general reasoning ability. But they are wrong.

The first step in coming to grips with math is to knock it off its pedestal. The real-life problems that are important to us are problems like these: Whom should I marry? Should I marry? Should gays be allowed to marry? What career should I go into and how should I prepare for it? If I invent gizmo X, will people buy it? Should corporations have the same constitutional rights as individuals? What's the best way to unplug the toilet? Math plays little if any role in solving such problems, nor do such problems have clear-cut right or wrong answers, demonstrable by some formula.

Human intelligence and reasoning reside in wisdom, not math. Wisdom is the ability to bring one's values, likes and dislikes, knowledge about other people and their likes and dislikes, and general knowledge of the world together in a manner that leads to workable solutions to the problems that confront us—solutions that promote our own and others' happiness and decrease our own and others' miseries. Math has its purposes, indeed it has some valuable purposes in our modern world, but it is far from the core of intelligence. Humans were intelligent long before math was invented. Some of the smartest people I know—even some of the best scientists I know—are not particularly good at math.

The second step in coming to grips with math is to realize that math is not particularly difficult. There is nothing magical about it. You do not need some natural gift beyond that of a normal human brain to do it. Nor does it require the thousands of hours of study that we try to force on school children. In fact, those thousands of hours of forced work at math, done for a grade and not for fun or for any practical use, are what make math seem so difficult and intimidating.

The best evidence I know that math is not hard comes from the experiences of people involved in the unschooling movement and the Sudbury democratic schooling movement. I have written about these movements in previous posts. Unschoolers are homeschooling families that do not provide a curriculum for their kids or evaluate their learning in any formal way. Sudbury schools are those that are modeled after the Sudbury Valley School, where kids of all ages are free all day to interact with whomever they choose and pursue their own interests. Unschoolers and Sudbury schoolers defy our cultural beliefs about what kids must do to succeed in our society. All available evidence shows that the kids in these settings grow up to become happy, productive, ethical members of the larger society, who continue to take charge of their own lives and learning throughout adulthood (Gray, 2017).

In order to learn more about the self-directed learning of math I invited parents of unschooling and democratic schooling children, through my *Psychology Today* blog, to send me stories about their children's self-directed learning of math. A total of 61 readers kindly responded, some with beautifully written pieces that could be stand-alone essays. I am extraordinarily grateful. Most of the stories came from unschooling parents. I spent several days conducting a qualitative analysis of these stories to extract common themes, which I summarize here.

I find it convenient to organize the stories into four categories based on the primary motive that seemed to underlie the math learning that was described. I have labeled the four categories as: playful math (math just for fun); instrumental math (math learned as a tool to solve problems encountered in daily life); didactic math (math studied according to some curriculum or plan set out by someone other than the learner, but still freely chosen by the learner); and college admissions math (math learned for the explicit purpose of performing well or adequately on the SAT, or ACT, or some other test used for college admissions). As I relay the stories about each of these categories of math learning my convention will be to use only the first names of the storytellers and not to use children's names at all, as some requested anonymity.

Playful Math

I've chosen to start, most joyfully, with playful math. Playful math might also be called "pure math." It is what real mathematicians do, and it is also what 4-year-olds do. Playful math is to numbers what poetry is to words, or music is to sounds, or art is to visual perception. I will write later about math that is used as a tool in play, but now I am writing about math that is play—math done for no other purpose than the sheer fun and beauty of it. Playful math involves the discovery or production of patterns in numbers, just as poetry involves the discovery or production of patterns in words, and music involves the discovery or production of patterns in sounds, and art involves the discovery or production of patterns in visual space.

Four-year-olds have a knack for bringing the whole world around them into the realm of play. They play with words, so they are poets. They play with sounds, so they are musicians. They play with crayons, paints, and clay, so they are artists. And they play with numbers, so they are mathematicians. I've noticed that students at Sudbury Valley, who are free of any imposed curriculum, don't stop such play as they grow older. They continue to play with words, sounds, paints, and numbers and often become really good at such play. The same seems to be true for kids growing up in unschooling homes.

The earliest math play, by little kids, commonly involves the discoveries that numbers come in a fixed sequence, that the sequence repeats itself in a regular (base-10) way, and that once you understand the pattern there is no end to how high you can count. Here are three quotations from unschoolers' stories that nicely illustrate this point:

Evelyn wrote, of her 4¾-year-old son (who "insists that the ¾ be included"): "When he found out about connect-the-dot drawings, it started to click for him how numbers proceed in order. He started counting aloud all the time, when walking, when lying in bed, etc. . . . The other day he was playing with one of his in-school friends, and her mother expressed shock that he did so well with the 'teen' numbers. . . . He counted to 30 for her in Spanish and then told her he could count to one million in English. So, since then, he has been counting morning, noon and night. This, as you can imagine, can sometimes be hard on others, and we have to remind ourselves it's a good thing! . . . He is now at 5,068. . . . And when I tell people he is counting to one million, he says, 'No, 10 million.' I hope I can survive it!"

Lucy, in the UK, wrote about her son who had just turned 5: "He counted to 100 once just for the fun of it whilst getting dressed. It was the first time I realized he could do that! He loves to line up number magnets and get me to tell him what the number is, particularly when the number goes into the millions! He can work out what a number is into the thousands from playing with fridge magnets. He has learned about odd and even numbers from walking around locally and noticing the numbers on houses. He can recognize them in other contexts now. He also learned to count in twos by predicting the next house number. We have never done any formal arithmetic or written anything down."

Kathy wrote: "Our oldest son, who is 6, has always been fascinated by numbers. He could count to 199 before the age of 4. He loved to count, and to have me count, and to do rhythmic things with his body. He would jump while I counted, or bounce on the couch. He started on math when he wanted to know how many things he would have if he doubled them. We went through a doubling phase!"

In their continued math play, young children often discover the basic concepts of adding, subtracting, multiplying, dividing, and more. Once they have the concepts, the actual ways of performing these operations come easily. Here are a few quotations from the many stories that reinforced this idea:

Janet wrote, of her young daughter: "She developed counting skills as most toddlers do, using fingers, food and toys, and game pieces and spaces on game boards and computer games. . . . That naturally led to adding and subtracting with fingers and objects, and then doing that in her head. . . . Often, seemingly out of the blue, she would ask questions like, 'Does four plus 10 equal 14?' Me: 'Yes.' She: 'Then does five plus 10 equal 15 and seven plus 10 equal 17?' She quickly found patterns in the adding and subtracting of numbers and would apply these rules, which she discovered on her own, and increase the values used. This genuine interest in the patterns numbers create was most noticeable in her seventh year. . . . I myself was quite terrified of math as a school child and teenager. But I have to say that [my experience watching and talking with my daughter] has given me a new appreciation for math and a sharpness of mind, with regard to calculations, that I had never previously felt. I also see real beauty in the unfolding of her relationship with numbers."

Unschooling mom Lori wrote: "One thing just happened two minutes ago. My younger son [age 5] was building with Legos while I was in another room, and he called out to me with a smile on his face, while jumping on the couch, 'Mom! What is four plus four plus four plus four?' I said, '16.' He smiled and said, 'What is eight plus eight?' I said, '16.' He smiled more and said, 'What is two plus two plus two. . .' and he got exactly the right number of twos to go to 16. It was clear that he knew the answers to these questions before he asked. These were not memorized from having been taught, but concepts that he figured out from working with Legos and playing around with the numbers in his head and on his fingers. And he was thrilled to manipulate the numbers, all on his own. To him, it was a game."

A-L wrote of her young son: "When he was 3 or 4, one day he went into our living room where we have a large window and noticed that there were four rows of seven panes. 'So,' he said, 'if I count to seven four times then it's 28.' I don't think we'd ever talked about multiplication at that point, but he'd essentially figured out how it worked and how to do it on his own from looking at the arrangement of squares. He began experimenting with it on his own, [putting] buttons in rows arrayed like the panes of glass. He still had to count up most of his answers because he hadn't committed them to memory, but he understood how it worked and what it meant."

Barbara wrote this about her unschooled young daughter: "She had just been telling me what games she and her friend had been playing, and then we were both quiet for several minutes. All of a sudden she exclaimed, quite excitedly, 'Oh, I get it!!!' I asked her what she meant, and she replied, 'I understand division.' . . . She then proceeded to explain that when you have a whole of something and you want to break it up into some number of equal parts, that's division. Then she asked me to quiz her, and she indeed knew how to do simple division. Before this moment we had never played around with division. I had never given her any problems to solve, nor had I even tried to explain what it was. . . . My story doesn't explain how she has learned these math concepts. But I do know that our lifestyle gives her the time to integrate, ponder, and wonder about the things she sees and hears in the world around her. In her own way, she gets to make the connections, puzzle things out, and test her theories. And I am certain that when she 'gets' something she will remember it and use it because it is truly her discovery."

Aurore wrote of her son: "One evening, at age 7, he had brought home a pack of Skittles. Like many kids, he likes to put them on a plate, sort them by color and play with them. On this day he had nine left and arranged them into three rows of three. He said, 'you know, the number nine is a square.' I told him that's what it's called, a square number, and that he could also make a square with four rows of four. He ended up making bigger and bigger squares . . . When it became impractical to keep making squares with Skittles (too big), or perhaps because he was just getting bored with doing that, he used a calculator to find more square numbers and wrote them down."

Some readers are no doubt thinking, "Well, a good teacher can use these sorts of demonstrations to teach math and thereby help children learn more quickly and efficiently than they could through self-discovery." But the problem with such reasoning is that every child is different and no teacher, no matter how brilliant, can get into every child's mind and come up with just the trick that will engage that mind at that exact time. That's why self-learning—learning in which the child is in charge—is almost always, in the long run, more efficient and enduring than anything that can be taught by even the most brilliant teacher to someone who hasn't taken charge of the process.

Instrumental Math

Math is not just play. It is also a useful instrument (tool) in our daily lives, and to that extent we naturally learn it in our daily lives. Most of the math stories sent to me included at least some account of learning math as a tool in daily living. Here are a few choice quotations from those stories:

Amy, a homeschooling mother of seven, wrote: "They all know how to divide and multiply, calculate percentages, add and subtract, just by handling money and cooking. I'm sure it helps that they have to share limited amounts of yummy snacks not only among the seven of them but with various friends who are always around. Food and money teach kids a LOT of math, and it highly motivates them."

Anne wrote: "All five kids learned to read recipes and how to divide or double or triple a recipe's ingredients. They read maps and figured out the mileage. They all played various card games and board games that use numbers and/or reasoning skills—Uno, Skip-bo, Pinochle, etc. As they became involved in local sports, they learned how to keep the scorebook and figure out averages. One son learned how to make a spreadsheet to keep track of his team's batting averages. They all kept their own ledgers in their bank savings accounts."

Vincente, a staff member at a Sudbury school, sent me this cute story: "Somehow we always end up with a lot of loose change, which needs to be rolled to be deposited. One of our very young students chose to do this [with my help]. We make stacks of five and count to 50, stack and roll. This is just the beginning; it gets better. . . . A week later I'm dodging vampires. Another of our mega-young invites me to play in one of the first role-playing adventures he's running. . . . The penny-counter and others are watching us, learning. The dungeon master rolls four fives in a dexterity check, his vampire executing a superb jump and spin landing on one hand on a pencil thin branch. Out of secondary hearing the penny-counter's words clink into the space reserved for Peter's blog: 'four times five is 20, five four times is 20.' Commutative property of multiplication—check."

And this, from Jennifer: "Three years ago, my son [at age 8] was diagnosed with Type 1 diabetes. Now, every meal is math. We calculate total carbohydrates from nutritional labels, total carbs for a meal, carb to insulin ratios by time of day, correction factors, percentages, etc. Now he NEEDS to know math to stay alive. He still hates memorizing times tables. . . . If I asked him, 'What is three times six?' I just got a blank stare. Then one day at lunch he wanted cookies, so I said, 'OK, if each cookie has six grams of carb and you are going to eat three, how much carb is that all together?' Without even blinking, he replied, '18.'"

But it's not just food and money. Here's another example:

Beatrice wrote: "Playing the piano, my daughter told me she was doing math. She was encountering fractions—half notes, quarter notes, eighth notes, sixteenth notes, all in musical notation as well as in patterns and rhythm."

Many of the stories sent to me about instrumental math had to do with games. Most of the games involve numbers, at least to keep score; and some of them involve really complicated math, which the players pick up eagerly in order to play the game. Here are a few representative quotations:

H wrote: "I have three kids attending a democratic free school with no imposed curriculum. My kids have spent a lot of time playing online games. Real games, not those stupid educational ones. My 11-year-old son plays MapleStory and has figured out complex mathematical structures to play the game. 'If I want to buy this helmet for this amount, how many hours do I have to play making this amount per hour in order to buy the helmet? If I sell this item in the market and the fee to sell is a certain percentage, how much will I have left after the fee? If I have this percentage of experience and I make a certain percentage per hour of experience, how many hours will it take to level up?' . . . Plus in the game you work with three different currencies and have to be able to translate back and forth among them regularly. Put these problems isolated from the game context to a bunch of 5th-graders in 'real' school and ask them to show their work and see what you get."

Rebecca wrote: "Before my oldest son was 'school age' he learned to solve basic math problems so that he could save the world from enemy invaders."

Gillian wrote: "My 10-year-old and 5-year-old are unschooled and there is no way to avoid them being exposed to math if they live a stimulating life. In particular, the computer and PS3 games that my son plays—World of Warcraft, Second Life, Uncharted, City of Heroes—have math concepts built into them in a completely natural way. I do not particularly like games that are deliberately 'educational' and my children have never liked them. Any time I have tried to direct them to those games they lose interest very quickly, perhaps because those games are often condescending in tone and less complex than a well-designed game. But give them intelligent games to play and almost inevitably they learn lots of things that schools try to cover in the school syllabus, and they learn them in a much more natural and effortless way."

And Erica wrote: "My sons (ages 11 and 7) made up a game together called 'Draw Fight.' It's a strategy game that uses addition and subtraction. Each of them draws their own character and . . . each character gets 50 points to spend at the beginning of the game towards his fighting skills, weapons, health, and armor. Choosing where to spend your points is very important because some of the things are worth more than others. After each player has had a turn to attack, you must add up your damage points done to the enemy character and subtract points that were taken from your character. The player with the most points remaining at the end of the game wins."

Beyond the world of food, games, and handling your own money, math is also an essential tool in some careers—such in physics, engineering, and accounting. People who freely choose such careers eagerly learn the math they need as part of their self-training, regardless of any deficiency in their previous math education. Here are three stories about math for careers:

Terry, a homeschooling (but not unschooling) mom, wrote: "My oldest always balked at math. . . . He fought me about doing any math workbooks and I started asking for less and less in the way of math. . . . We stopped after 5th grade. He had always enjoyed pretty much unlimited computer time and enjoyed writing games and programs in a self-taught way. He was offered [at age 17] an internship doing programming at a company that auctions municipal bonds. He did so well that they hired him and he is still working there at age 20. He really has a knack for programming and finds the bond and tax stuff fascinating. He is often on the phone with big-time bank executives who have no idea that they are talking to someone so young. He still can't tell you what six times seven is without having to add it in his head. He took placement tests to get into community college and did badly on the math part and was supposed to take a remedial math class. This bothered him because you have to pay to take the remedial math, but you don't get credit for it. So . . . he did two days of math study and re-took the test. This time he placed out of both the remedial math and the basic math courses. If he sees a reason to learn something, he will do it. Otherwise, forget it!"

Dan, a Ph.D. candidate in anthropology, wrote to me explaining that the out-of-context math courses he took in college left him poorly trained for the statistics he needed in his graduate work. He added: "Through a lot of self-teaching and a little mentorship, I am [now] better at statistics than most of the professors I encounter."

A colleague of mine, a highly esteemed biologist whose work includes the development of mathematical models, wrote in an autobiographical sketch that he performed poorly in math in high school and college and learned little. He wrote: "I took one year of math in college, freshman calculus, and it almost killed me. In graduate school I had strong reason to learn math so I did. I purchased *Calculus for Dummies*, practiced hard, and pestered more knowledgeable graduate students when I got stuck. It wasn't exactly fun, but every time I figured something out I had a feeling of triumph that motivated me to take the next step. I published my first theoretical paper while still a graduate student and now I'm a well-known theoretical biologist."

Didactic Math

If this were a typical article about math education, it would be entirely about didactic math—math as it is taught by educators to students. Our society is so convinced that this is how math must be learned that even parents who become unschoolers are often reluctant, at first, to give up the formal or semi-formal teaching of math. They tend, for awhile, to succumb to the cultural beliefs that (a) math knowledge is essential for success in our society and (b) math is no fun, so most people will not learn it on their own. But over time, watching their kids, they change their minds and stop the instruction. Here is a quotation that nicely expresses these points:

Rebecca wrote: "With my son's apparent agreement, we succumbed to using a packaged program, with a video component. . . . And then it happened. Both my son and I lost our enthusiasm. He was bored. I didn't like the way things were going in the material . . . repetition, repetition, and more repetition. So, after internal writhing, I pried my white-knuckled hands from the crutch of the packaged, predictable, lock-step curriculum and told my son that I was done with my part in making that happen. . . . Letting go of the math curriculum (and expectations) has been a huge weight off of my mind. For so many years I had a split home-learning personality—'we unschool, except in math.' I was all tied up in knots about math and felt I had to strongly encourage (coerce?) my son to adopt a traditional approach to learning it." Rebecca went on to explain that her initial concern for teaching math had to do with expectations about college. For years she couldn't let go of the idea that her son must attend college to have a good life and he must learn math in order to get into college (even though he was not yet 9 years old).

A number of other respondents pointed out that math lessons and programs are easy for kids who choose to do them and are allowed to do them in their own ways, on their own schedules. Here are several quotations to that effect:

Carlotta, from the UK, wrote, about her son who did no formal math lessons until age 12: "He then shot through Key Stage 3 Maths in about three weeks of doing just a little bit here and there. He found it almost ridiculously easy, doing things like memorizing his tables (with some interest in the various patterns that he spotted) in less than an hour. Trigonometry easy peasy, equations no problem. . . . OK, so he had spent a considerable amount of his younger years playing the markets on Runescape and solving other mathematical problems in various (fun) games . . . but that had been it. SOO much less sweat."

Fawn wrote: "My 11-year-old daughter was homeschooled for grades 2-5. We did very little formal math instruction, maybe an hour a week total. She had a workbook she could do when she felt like it, and if she had a question I would briefly explain, but she was pretty much on her own. At the end of 4th grade she scored way above grade level on a standardized math test. She is now in sixth grade in a traditional school, at her request, and she has a 94 average in math."

Leslie wrote: "We did some hands-on stuff, but honestly, I was handicapped by my own math education to the point that when I would try to explain to my kids how to do something, one of them would interrupt me and say, 'you're confusing me—this is how I do it' and then explain some much more elegant way of coming to the right answer that showed me that they had a much better understanding of HOW math worked than I ever did. It always humbled me."

An anonymous commenter on my last post wrote: "One friend of mine was an unschooler and the extent of her son's math education was reading Murderous Maths when he felt like it. At 14 he decided he'd like to take algebra at the community college. He picked up a textbook and learned all of arithmetic in a few weeks. Another friend put her son into school at fifth grade. After the testing the school said her son would never be at grade level by the end of the year. He caught up in a month."

College Admission Math

And now, finally, we come to the math that middle-class parents most worry about. For some odd reason we have decided, as a society, that all young people who go to college—even those who want to become poets or linguists—must show their mettle on a test of ability to do a certain amount of algebra, geometry, and trigonometry that they will never do again. And so, some companies make lots of money tutoring kids—kids who have already "taken" thousands of hours of math in school—to do those tests. And quite often the tutoring does the trick, because the young people at this point want to learn what they must to get into the college of their choice. Then they can promptly forget, forever, the math that they had put into their temporary memory banks. Here are two pieces about how unschooled kids prepare for the math SAT or ACT.

Leslie wrote this about her son who was entirely unschooled until he went to college: "The first real formal math he did was when he studied for the ACT test. When he was younger, we had math workbooks and even a couple textbooks around the house, but they barely got looked at. . . .The 'dirty little secret' about math is that it just doesn't take as long to learn it as we're culturally indoctrinated to believe it takes. My son learned enough math in just a few weeks to get a 33 on the ACT test just by studying some ACT test prep books." [Note: In the United States, the ACT is most commonly used in the middle states and the SAT is most commonly used on and near the two coasts.]

To find out more about how kids with no formal math training deal with college admissions math, I interviewed Mikel Matisoo, the Sudbury Valley staff member who is most often sought out by students who want help in preparing for the math SAT. He told me that the kids who come to him are usually those who have relatively little genuine interest in math; they just want to do well enough on the SAT to get into the college of their choice. He said, "The way the SAT is structured it is relatively easy to prepare directly for it; there are certain tricks for doing well." Typically, Mikel meets with the students for about one to one and a half hours per week for about six to 10 weeks and the students may do another one to one and a half hours per week on their own. That amounts to a range of about 12 to 30 hours, total, of math work for kids who may never before have done any formal math. The typical result, according to Mikel, is a math SAT score that is good enough for admission to at least a moderately competitive college. Mikel explained that the kids who are really into math, and who get the top SAT scores, generally don't seek him out because they can prepare on their own.

And so, parents, you don't need to worry about your kids' learning of math. If they are free to play, they are likely to play with math and learn to enjoy its patterns. If they live real lives that involve calculations, they will learn, in their own unique ways, precisely the calculations that they need to live those lives. If they choose to go to college, they can learn quickly—from a test preparation book, computer program, or tutorial—the specific math tricks necessary to do well enough on college admissions math. If they choose some career that involves math, they will eagerly find ways to learn the specific kinds of math that they need for that career. Your worry is only a hindrance.

6

Facts and Fiction About the So-Called "Summer Slide"

Do children really learn less during summer vacation? Less of what?

JULY 22, 2017

Every summer we hear from educators about the "summer slide" in academic learning. The claim is that children lose much of what they gained from school during the summer break, so time is lost catching up in the fall. Some even argue that school should continue through the summer, so as to prevent that loss! Here are a few questions and thoughts that come to my mind whenever I hear about the summer slide:

If children lose academic skills over the few weeks of summer, then did they really ever learn those skills? It must have been pretty shallow learning.

If the skills taught in school are lost so easily, then what happens when people finally finish school and go on to life outside of it? Won't the skills be lost then? If we're going to force children to stay in school all summer so they don't lose skills, then maybe we should force all of us to stay in school our whole lives, so we don't lose skills!

Very often people writing about the summer slide seem to assume that the only learning that is important is that which occurs in school and is measured on academic tests. It's amazing to me how often this assumption goes unchallenged. As I've argued in my book *Free to Learn* and in many essays in this series, the most important lessons of life cannot be taught and can only be learned through real life experiences. In real life we learn how to make our own decisions, create our own activities, actually DO things as opposed to memorize things. For schoolchildren, summer is a time for immersion in real life. School, at best, prepares children for more school. Real life prepares children for real life.

The claims about the summer slide led me to be curious about the data. What does research actually reveal concerning a loss of school learning over the summer? I spent a couple days digging into the research literature, and what I found suggests that much of what we hear about the summer slide is myth.

Research relevant to the summer slide has been going on for about 100 years. Most of the studies referred to by advocates of school through the summer were conducted decades ago (for a review, see Cooper et al., 1996); so I went back and looked at those studies. Most of them focused just on reading and mathematics abilities. Although the results are somewhat inconsistent from study to study, most studies show either no significant change or an average increase in reading ability over the summer. The concern seems to be with mathematics, where quite a few studies show a significant decline. That got me curious. Are all kinds of math abilities lost or only some?

Math calculation declines but math reasoning increases over the summer.

I found three research studies in which students were tested just before and just after summer vacation with math achievement tests that separated calculation ability from math reasoning ability. Two of them showed that calculation scores declined over the summer, but all three of them showed that math reasoning scores increased quite substantially over the summer. This should be no surprise.

Calculation tests assess the ability to add, subtract, multiply, and divide without error. A typical easy question might be, What is 58 plus 44? A harder question might be, What is 5/8 divided by 1/2? Students in school generally learn the procedures for doing such calculations by rote, without necessarily understanding why you do it that way. Material learned by rote is pretty easily lost when it isn't rehearsed. Today, of course, hardly anyone does such calculations outside of school; we all have calculators or computers.

Math reasoning tests assess students' understanding of math concepts and their ability to use those concepts to solve problems. This, of course, requires much deeper knowledge than the rote memory needed for calculations. A typical easy question might be, How do you determine the area of a rectangle? Or, a harder question might be, If a gallon of paint covers 200 square feet, how much paint do you need to cover all four walls of a room that is 20 feet long, 15 feet wide, and 9 feet high? This question does require some calculation, but first you have to figure out what it is you need to calculate.

Here are the findings of the three studies that separated calculation and reasoning.

Parsely & Powell (1962) tested students in grades 1-6 in public schools in Ohio at the end of the academic year and again at the beginning of the next. For the calculation test (called "fundamentals") they found a somewhat different pattern of change for each grade level, but, overall, there was no significant gain or loss over the summer. For the reasoning test, most grades showed a significant gain over the summer. When I calculated the average gain in math reasoning, for all grades combined, it amounted to a grade equivalent of 0.24. Stated differently, they gained as much during summer vacation weeks as they would be expected to gain in a quarter of a year. The biggest gain—0.55 grade equivalent—was shown by the sixth-graders.

Grenier (1973) tested seventh-graders in public junior high schools in Griffin, Georgia, at the end of the academic year, and then re-tested some of them at the very beginning of the next academic year and others two weeks later. Her math test consisted of three components: computation, concepts, and applications. For my purposes, here, I combined the concepts and applications scores, to produce a math reasoning score. Here are Grenier's results: For computations she found a grade equivalent decline of 0.22 year for those tested immediately at the end of vacation, but a grade equivalent increase of 0.10 year for those tested two weeks later. So, there was a summer slide in computation, but that loss was more than regained within two weeks back at school. For reasoning she found an average grade equivalent increase of 0.48 year. In other words, during the three months of summer vacation they gained nearly half a year in math reasoning ability.

Wintre (1986) tested Toronto elementary school students in grades one, three, and five at the end of the school year and, again, at the beginning of the next school year. I can't compare her findings directly with those of the other studies, because she reported only the mean raw scores on each test and did not show a conversion to grade equivalency. But the pattern of her results was the same as that for the other two studies. Combining all grades, she found a significant increase (+5.4 percent in mean score) for math reasoning and a small decrease (-1.7 percent) for computation. She also tested word knowledge and reading comprehension and (as in many other studies) found significant increases in both of those, of +5.2 percent and +6.2 percent, respectively.

Which is more important, the ability to perform calculations accurately by hand (which nobody in the real world does any more) or the ability to understand the meanings of mathematical concepts and to apply them to real problems? The former ability increases more rapidly during the school year than during the summer; the latter increases more rapidly during the summer than during the school year.

So, take away summer, and we will produce lots of graduates who know how to do calculations but have no idea why anyone would do them other than to pass a test. But then, of course, they will forget how to do the calculations by a few weeks after graduation, as that is what is lost when not in school.

Maybe instead of expanding the school year to reduce a summer slide in calculation we should expand summer vacation to reduce the school-year slide in reasoning.

References

Cooper, H., et al. (1996). The effects of summer vacation on achievement test scores: A narrative and meta-analytic review. *Review of Educational Research*, 66, 227-268.

Grenier, M. A. (1975). An investigation of summer mathematics achievement loss and the related fall recovery time. Doctoral dissertation, University of Georgia. Available from ProQuest Dissertations and Theses.

Parsley, K. M., & Powell, M. (1962). Achievement gains or losses during the academic year and over the summer vacation period: A study of trends in achievement by sex and grade level among students of average intelligence. *Genetic Psychology Monographs*, 66, 285-342.

Wintre, M. G. (1986). Challenging the assumption of generalized academic losses over summer. *Journal of Educational Research*, 79, 308-312.

7

Early Academic Training Produces Long-Term Harm

Research reveals negative effects of academic preschools and kindergartens

MAY 5 AND JUNE 3, 2015

Many preschool and kindergarten teachers have told me that they are extremely upset—some to the point of being ready to resign—by the increased pressure on them to teach academic skills to little children and regularly test them on such skills. They can see firsthand the unhappiness generated, and they suspect that the children would be learning much more useful lessons through playing, exploring, and socializing, as they did in traditional nursery schools and kindergartens. Their suspicions are well validated by research.

A number of well-controlled studies have compared the effects of academically oriented early education classrooms with those of play-based classrooms (some of which are reviewed by Carlsson-Paige et al., 2015). The results are quite consistent from study to study: Early academic training somewhat increases children's immediate scores on the specific tests that the training is aimed at (no surprise), but these initial gains wash out within one to three years and, at least in some studies, are eventually reversed. Perhaps more tragic than the lack of long-term academic advantage of early academic instruction is evidence that such instruction can produce long-term harm, especially in social and emotional development, but also even in academic learning.

A Study in Germany that Changed Educational Policy There

For example, in the 1970s, the German government sponsored a large-scale comparison in which the graduates of 50 play-based kindergartens were compared, over time, with the graduates of 50 academic direct-instruction-based kindergartens (Darling-Hammond & Snyder, 1992). Despite the initial academic gains of direct instruction, by grade four the children from the direct-instruction kindergartens performed significantly worse than those from the play-based kindergartens on every measure that was used. They were less advanced in reading and mathematics and less well adjusted socially and emotionally. At the time of the study, Germany was gradually switching from traditional play-based kindergartens to academic ones. At least partly as a result of the study, Germany reversed that trend; they went back to play-based kindergartens. Apparently, German educational authorities, at least at that time, unlike American authorities today, actually paid attention to educational research and used it to inform educational practice.

A Large-Scale Study of Children from Poverty in the United States

Similar studies in the United States have produced comparable results. One study, directed by Rebecca Marcon (2002), focused on mostly African American children from high-poverty families. As expected, she found—in her sample of 343 students—that those who attended preschools centered on academic training showed initial academic advantages over those who attended play-based preschools; but, by the end of fourth grade, these initial advantages were reversed: The children from the play-based preschools were now performing better, getting significantly higher school grades, than those from the academic preschool. This study included no assessment of social and emotional development.

An Experiment in Which Children from Poverty Were Followed up to Age 23

In a well-controlled experiment, begun by David Weikart and his colleagues in 1967, 68 high-poverty children living in Ypsilanti, Michigan, were assigned to one of three types of nursery schools: Traditional (play-based), High/Scope (which was like the traditional but involved more adult guidance), and Direct Instruction (where the focus was on teaching reading, writing, and math, using worksheets and tests). The assignment was done in a semi-random way, designed to ensure that the three groups were initially matched on all available measures. In addition to the daily preschool experiences, the experiment also included a home visit every two weeks, aimed at instructing parents in how to help their children. These visits focused on the same sorts of methods as did the preschool classrooms. Thus, home visits from the Traditional classrooms focused on the value of play and socialization while those from the Direct-Instruction classrooms focused on academic skills, worksheets, and the like.

The initial results of this experiment were similar to those of other such studies. Those in the direct-instruction group showed early academic gains, which soon vanished. This study, however, also included follow-up research when the participants were 15 years old and again when they were 23 years old. At these ages there were no significant differences among the groups in academic achievement, but large, significant differences in social and emotional characteristics.

By age 15 those in the Direct Instruction group had committed, on average, more than twice as many "acts of misconduct" than had those in the other two groups. At age 23, as young adults, the differences were even more dramatic. Those in the Direct Instruction group had more instances of friction with other people, were more likely to have shown evidence of emotional impairment, were less likely to be married and living with their spouse, and were far more likely to have committed a crime than were those in the other two groups. In fact, by age 23, 39 percent of those in the Direct Instruction group had felony arrest records compared to an average of 13.5 percent in the other two groups; and 19 percent of the Direct Instruction group had been cited for assault with a dangerous weapon compared with 0 percent in the other two groups (Schweinhart & Weikart, 1997).

What might account for such dramatic long-term effects of type of preschool attended? One possibility is that the initial school experience sets the stage for later behavior. Those in classrooms where they learned to plan their own activities, to play with others, and to negotiate differences may have developed lifelong patterns of personal responsibility and pro-social behavior that served them well throughout their childhood and early adulthood. Those in classrooms that emphasized academic performance may have developed lifelong patterns aimed at achievement, and getting ahead, which—especially in the context of poverty—could lead to friction with others and even to crime (as a misguided means of getting ahead).

I suspect that the biweekly home visits played a meaningful role. The parents of those in the classrooms that focused on play, socialization, and student initiative may have developed parenting styles that continued to reinforce those values and skills as the children were growing up, and the parents of those in the academic training group may have developed parenting styles more focused on personal achievement (narrowly defined) and self-centered values—values that did not bode well for real-world success.

Why Intellectual Skills Must Precede
Academic Skills for Meaningful Learning

To understand why early academic training can inhibit academic performance years later it is valuable to distinguish between academic skills and intellectual skills—a distinction nicely made in an article by Lillian Katz (2015).

Academic skills are tried and true means of organizing, manipulating, or responding to specific categories of information to achieve certain ends. Pertaining to reading, for example, academic skills include the abilities to name the letters of the alphabet, to produce the sounds that each letter typically stands for, and to read words aloud, including new ones, based on the relationship of letters to sounds. Pertaining to mathematics, academic skills include the abilities to recite the times table and to add, subtract, multiply, and divide numbers using learned, step-by-step procedures, or algorithms. Academic skills can be and are taught directly in schools, through methods involving demonstration, recitation, memorization, and repeated practice. Such skills lend themselves to objective tests, in which each question has one right answer.

Intellectual skills, in contrast, have to do with a person's ways of reasoning, hypothesizing, exploring, understanding, and, in general, making sense of the world. Every child is, by nature, an intellectual being—a curious, sense-making person, who is continuously seeking to understand his or her physical and social environments. Each child is born with such skills and develops them further, in his or her own ways, through observing, exploring, playing, and questioning. Attempts to teach intellectual skills directly inevitably fail, because each child must develop them in his or her own way, through his or her own self-initiated activities. But adults can influence that development through the environments they provide. Children growing up in a literate and numerate environment, for example—such as an environment in which they are often read to and see others read, in which they play games that involve numbers, and in which things are measured for real-world purposes—will acquire, in their own ways, understandings of the purposes of reading and the basic meaning and purposes of numbers.

Now, here's the point to which I'm leading. It is generally a waste of time, and often harmful, to teach academic skills to children who have not yet developed the requisite motivational and intellectual foundations. Children who haven't acquired a reason to read or a sense of its value will have little motivation to learn the academic skills associated with reading and little understanding of those skills. Similarly, children who haven't acquired an understanding of numbers and how they are useful may learn the procedure for, say, addition, but that procedure will have little or no meaning to them.

The learning of academic skills without the appropriate intellectual foundation is necessarily shallow. When the drill stops—maybe for summer vacation—the skills are quickly forgotten. (That's the famous "summer slide" in academic ability that some educators want to reduce by keeping children in school all year long!) Our brains are designed to hold onto what we understand and to discard nonsense. Moreover, when the procedures are learned by rote, especially if the learning is slow, painful, and shame-inducing, as it often is when forced, such learning may interfere with the intellectual development needed for real reading or real math.

Rote-trained, pained children may lose all desire to play with and explore literary and numerical worlds on their own and thereby fail to develop the intellectual foundations for real reading or math. This explains why researchers repeatedly find that academic training in preschool and kindergarten results in worse, not better, performance on academic tests in later grades. This is also why children's advocacy groups—such as Defending the Early Years and the Alliance for Childhood—are so strongly opposed to the current trend of teaching academic skills to ever-younger children. The early years, especially, should be spent playing, exploring, and developing the intellectual foundations that will allow children to acquire academic skills relatively easily later on.

This distinction between academic and intellectual skills also helps us make sense of some of the research findings discussed in previous essays in this volume. As already noted, it explains why children in standard schools lose, over summer vacation, some of the abilities to perform rote mathematical calculations that they memorized during the school year but generally improve in their understanding of mathematical procedures and ability to apply those procedures to real-world problems (essay 5). It also helps us make sense of Benezet's finding that children not taught any mathematics until sixth grade performed better on math story problems by the end of that grade than did those who began their math training much earlier (essay 3). The children who were taught early learned the academic math skills by rote, and this interfered with the kind of intellectual understanding of numbers and calculations needed to solve story problems.

And, most crucial for the theme of this volume, this distinction between academic and intellectual skills helps explain why unschooled children and children in schools for Self-Directed Education, such as Sudbury Valley, learn to read and to calculate so easily when they decide to do so (essays 2 and 4). Because their learning takes place in the real world, where reading and numerical calculation are meaningful, they acquire the intellectual understandings and motives for reading and calculating first, so the academic skills make sense to them and are learned in a deep rather than shallow way.

References

Carlsson-Paige, N., McLaughlin, G. B., & Almon, J. W. (2015). Reading instruction in kindergarten: Little to gain and much to lose. Published online by the Alliance for Childhood. http://www.allianceforchildhood.org/sites/allianceforchildhood.org/files/file/Reading_Instruction_in_Kindergarten.pdf

Darling-Hammond, L., & Snyder, J. 1992. Curriculum studies and the traditions of inquiry: The scientific tradition. In P. W. Jackson (Ed.), *Handbook of research on curriculum*, pp 41-78. MacMillan.

Katz, L. G. (2015). Lively minds: Distinctions between academic versus intellectual goals for young children. Defending the Early Years (DEY). Available online at https://deyproject.files.wordpress.com/2015/04/dey-lively-minds-4-8-15.pdf

Marcon, R. A. (2002). Moving up the grades: Relationship between preschool model and later school success. *Early Childhood Research & Practice, 4,* 517-530.

Schweinhart, L. J., & Weikart, D. P. (1997). The high/scope preschool curriculum comparison study through age 23. *Early Childhood Research Quarterly 12,* 117-143.

8

K and Preschool Teachers

Last Stand in War on Childhood?

*Kindergarten and preschool teachers
everywhere are struggling to preserve play*

JULY 8, 2015

The war against childhood continues. Children are no longer generally free to roam, play, and explore on their own, as they were in the past and are designed to do by nature. Parents who allow such play are sometimes arrested. Schools throughout the country have eliminated or greatly curtailed recesses.

The last bastion in the battle to preserve childhood appears to be preschools and kindergartens, where some play still exists. But ground is quickly being lost there, too, despite the efforts of many teachers to hold on.

I have spoken in recent months at several conferences of early childhood educators, mostly preschool and kindergarten teachers. At each, I've heard passionate descriptions of struggles to preserve play. They are battling the effects of No

Child Left Behind, and now Common Core, which have trickled down from the higher grades to K and preschool. They are battling policy makers who know nothing about childhood, who ignore the piles of research showing the value of play and the long-term harm of early academic training and who see standardized test scores as the end-all and be-all of education. They are battling administrators, who either have fallen for the pro-testing propaganda or are cynically pretending they believe it in order to preserve their high-salaried positions. They are battling teachers in the grades above, who tell them that their job is to prepare little children for the next stage in school by teaching them to sit still, do worksheets, and suppress their urges to play and explore. They are battling parents, who have come to believe that their 3-, 4-, and 5-year-olds will never get into Harvard if they "just play" in preschool and kindergarten. Sometimes the battle is too hard, so they quit, or worse: they give in and do what they know is wrong. [Note: Early childhood educators as a whole are loving and nonviolent people, so when I say "battle," I am referring to their attempts at reasoned persuasion.]

Some Comments from Early Childhood Educators on My Last Two Essays

In my last two essays in this series (posted May 5 and June 3, 2015), I summarized some of the evidence and logic behind the claim that the push toward early academic training is actually reducing, not increasing, academic ability in the long run and is damaging children's social and emotional development. Some of the most passionate comments on those essays came from preschool and kindergarten teachers. Here are quotations from five such commenters:

"I teach kindergarten for 11 more days. What we are doing to the 4- to 6-year-old kids in this country is absolutely unethical and inappropriate. Any professional educator who truly understands how children develop—academically, cognitively, socially, emotionally—will stand up against the travesty that reformers refer to as 'rigor.' Kids do NOT need to be reading by the end of kindergarten. (If they can, GREAT!) They do NOT need to be solving paper-and-pencil equations. They do NOT need to be doing 'academic' workstations. They DO need to be playing, painting, building, creating, interacting with books, listening to stories, singing songs, taking field trips, playing pretend, exploring, etc. . . . I am leaving kindergarten, but I will be fighting for early childhood so that I can eventually go back to kindergarten. I refuse to be part of something so dangerous to our young children."

"I am a retired preschool teacher. I taught young children for well over 20 years. I was always forced by my employers to push math, and especially writing, with 3-year-olds. The outcome of that push to academics was rarely successful and produced lots of miserable little people. I always believed that I was doing far more harm than good. I feel refreshed to read about experts who are trying to step out of that discipline of thinking. I hope that soon little ones will be able to go to preschool to play, have fun, and learn in a natural and happy way."

"The system as a whole is broken; it is why I left the profession. Truth is, most school districts, at least the ones I have worked in in America, do not use scientific evidence or best practices to teach kids. They instead use the next fad that comes along, 'Common Core' being the latest debacle, from government bureaucracy because it comes with money or grants from the state or federal government, and then test these kids to death until they hate school, hate learning, and wish nothing more than to get out because the ones that already are disadvantaged never measure up and continuously keep seeing their failures rather than their strengths. Worse, they test these kids in kindergarten, so the cycle of failure and frustration begins at an early age! If we want to change the education system, then it is up to the parents and educators who must stop allowing politicians and book companies, who make ridiculous amounts of money off these curriculum initiatives, to force these unscientific methods of teaching down the throats of children. Boycott testing, write your representatives, and go to School Board meetings and demand the reversal of early academic testing. It is the only way to bring play back to schools."

"As a preschool and Kindergarten teacher and trainer for over 30 years, I've seen such drastic changes in early childhood education—so many programs have gone from play based to skills based and the kids are losing out. . . . I've visited K programs where recess is no longer an option because 'the kids have so much work to do'!! I've been in classrooms where young students sit at their desks and cry because they can't do the writing the teacher is asking them to do."

It's not just in the US that this is occurring. Here's a comment from the UK:

I have been a primary school teacher (elementary) in the UK for the past 25 years. In that time, I have witnessed swings towards child-initiated learning and then all the way back again to didactic instruction. Our government sends in inspectors to check that we're following the latest dogma. As a result, we have the most tested children in the world. All children in England take a test at age 6 to check their phonics knowledge. Parents are informed if their child fails. Yes, you can be labeled a failure at the age of 6!"

Results of a "Netnographic" Study of Kindergarten Teachers' Views

Megham Lynch (2015) has published an interesting article describing her netnographic study of kindergarten teachers' writings about play in the classroom. Netnography is a new variety of ethnography that relies on the analysis of publicly available comments in social media to learn about the views and practices of a group of people. Lynch identified 78 distinct discussions by kindergarten teachers about play and academic training in kindergarten, on seven online teacher message boards, and analyzed them qualitatively. She found that almost all of the teachers agreed about the benefits of play for children and that most expressed concern about the conflict between children's needs for play and the pressure to restrict play in order to teach academic skills.

Pressures from "The System," i.e. from Mandated Policies

Many teachers explained that, because of policies mandated by NCLB and Common Core, they have no time for play in their classroom. They reported feeling overwhelmed by the attempts to raise the academic skills of little children who aren't ready for such skills. Teachers further lamented that there is no time even for traditional activities beyond play— "no more time for show and tell, no time for holiday and special crafts projects, not enough time for daily music and movement activities, the list goes on." Some feared that snack time was going to be taken away, because, as one put it, "it takes at least 10 minutes and with our new math mandated 70 minutes per day, there just is not time."

Pressures from Principals

The system, of course, funnels its way to teachers by way of superintendents and principals. Lynch found that principals were very frequently mentioned, usually is a negative light, in the discussions she analyzed. For example, one teacher wrote, "My principal said, 'They are not in kindergarten to color and play.'" Another wrote, "My new principal was appalled to see housekeeping centers and blocks. I got in trouble because I was completing mandatory individual testing on the sixth day of school and let my kids play with math manipulatives for 20 minutes while I did this."

Another teacher described how, when she was moved to a

new classroom, the principal threw away her entire closet full of play materials, despite the teacher's protest. Still another wrote about how she had the kids sitting on the floor singing "Farmer in the Dell" when the superintendent walked in and said, "You are going to stop singing and start teaching, right?"

Those teachers whose principals or superintendents allowed some play in kindergarten spoke of themselves as "lucky" and worried about what would happen if that person were replaced. One, for example, wrote, "I am blessed to have an assistant superintendent of elementary ed with an early-childhood background. She is extremely supportive of developmentally appropriate kindergarten classrooms."

Pressures from Other Teachers

Some kindergarten teachers said they felt looked down upon by the teachers of the higher grades if they allowed their students to play, or sing, or do other nonacademic things. One wrote, "One of our K teachers was made fun of by other teachers because the kids sang too much." Another wrote, "I will never forget the first-grade teacher telling me that by January our whole day should be spent in our seats doing paper-and-pencil activities to prepare them for first grade."

Pressures from Parents

Yet another source of pressure the kindergarten teachers described is parents. For example, one teacher wrote, "So many preschools build up a lot of hype about how academic they are in an effort to entice parents to send their children to their preschool. They give parents the wrong message. It confuses parents when their children come into kindergarten and they see the kitchen area and blocks. . . . The parents think their children aren't learning if they aren't doing paper-and-pencil tasks."

Fighting the Pressures

Many of the teachers described themselves as "battling" their administrators in order to preserve play. They said they were continuing to allow play in their classrooms, even though doing so got them repeatedly into trouble with the school administration. One wrote, as advice to another, "I've considered myself a bit of a rebel during all of the foolishness that's been going on in our state and in our classrooms for the past few years. I hope you will not buckle under the pressure—even though currently it is very scary to 'buck the system.' If we don't stay strong, though, the system is going to beat us down."

Some reported an end-run approach: To preserve some play they used labels designed to replace "the p word" with terms that sounded academic. They might retain their old play corner in the room by calling it a "developmental center," or "work center," or "active learning center"—anything but play! Along this same line, one special ed teacher managed to retain nap time by relabeling it "Sensory Differentiation Time"!

Before ending, I should note, not all of the kindergarten

teachers in Lynch's study supported the retention of play. Those teachers are yet another pressure working against the teachers who wish to retain play. One teacher wrote that teachers who permit play are simply being "lazy." Of course, the selective process of hiring and firing teachers to fit the horrible guidelines is going to increase the number of anti-play kindergarten teachers over time. How sad it will be when nobody remembers that children once played.

Reference

Lynch, M. (2015). More play please: The perspective of kindergarten teachers on play in the classroom. *American Journal of Play*, 7, 347-370.

9

Mend the Gap Between Rich and Poor in School Achievement

We know how to reduce the school achievement gap, but we do the opposite

SEPTEMBER 20, 2017

Our compulsory public school system is supposed to be "the great equalizer." By providing the same schooling to everyone, it is supposed to promote equal opportunities for young people regardless of their socioeconomic background. In fact, however, the system has never been a great equalizer, and research indicates that it is even much less an equalizer today than it was in the past.

A few years ago, Sean Reardon (2012) of Stanford University published an analysis of the findings of many studies showing, over all, that the gap in achievement test scores between students from the richest 10 percent of families and the poorest 10 percent grew by 40 to 50 percent between the mid 1970s and the early 2000s. The gap exists at all grade levels, but is much larger in the later years of schooling than in the early years. By the middle of high school, the average test scores for students from the bottom 10 percent in income are three to six grade levels (depending on the type of test) below those of students from the top 10 percent in income.

Here I'll describe some unsuccessful and successful attempts to reduce the achievement gap, and then I'll explain why I think public support for Self-Directed Education would be a great way to reduce or even eliminate the gap.

Some Failed Attempts to Reduce the Gap
More money spent on schooling
hasn't solved the problem.

Over the past few decades, federal, state, and local governments have greatly increased their spending for public education, at rates far exceeding inflation, and have decreased the spending gap between poor and rich school districts. Over those same decades, the achievement gap has increased. Indeed, research indicates that the average gap between rich and poor kids who are attending the same school, even in wealthy districts, is nearly as great as that between rich and poor kids who are attending different schools (Deruy, 2016; Tucker, 2007; Schmidt et al., 2015).

Reducing class size hasn't solved the problem.

One might think that with smaller classes teachers would give more individual attention to those students who need the most help, which would reduce the gap. However, research to date shows little or no relationship of class size either to overall student achievement or to the size of the gap between rich and poor (e.g. Hoxby, 2000; Cho et al, 2012). In fact, those few studies that do show increased achievement for smaller classes generally reveal that rich students benefit more than do poor ones (Jackson & Page, 2013; Li & Konstantopoulos, 2017). Perhaps reduced class size leads teachers to spend even more time with the high achieving students, while still neglecting the needier ones.

More pressure, drill, testing, and
standardization hasn't solved the problem.

The "No Child Left Behind" act and, more recently, the "Every Child Succeeds" act were designed, in part, to reduce the achievement gap. These programs, in theory, would reduce the differences among schools and among teachers in how they taught and would ensure that all students are subject to essentially the same curriculum and experience the same pressures to succeed in school. However, over the period that these programs have been in effect, the gap has increased.

Elsewhere, I have explained why this result should have been predictable (Gray, 2013). Many research studies have shown that high pressure improves performance for those who are already skilled at a task and worsens it for those who aren't skilled. The best way to learn something new is to learn it in a playful, non-stressful environment. If economically poor students start school knowing less of what is taught in schools than do rich ones, then high pressure would decrease their scores and increase those of the rich. Moreover, standardization in teaching and testing reduces the opportunity for teachers to respond differently to the needs of different students, so it would likely result in neglect of the real needs of economically poor students.

Starting academic training at younger
ages hasn't solved the problem.

Another failed approach to reducing the achievement gap has been to start teaching academic skills earlier—in kindergarten and even in pre-kindergarten. As I have documented earlier in this volume, these programs have generally produced short-term benefits, if benefits are measured as improved test scores in first grade, but have produced long-term harm, as measured by academic test scores and social skills assessments in later years. The early learning promoted by academic training in preschool and kindergarten is apparently shallow and not founded on intellectual understanding, so it interferes with deeper learning of literary and mathematical skills later on.

The gap decreases when "school climate" improves.

Another approach to school reform—quite opposite to that of increased pressure, drill, and standardization—is that of improving "school climate." Climate here refers to the attitudes that permeate a school's culture. A positive climate is one where teachers are warm, supportive, trustful, and respect-ful toward students as unique individuals and where students feel supported, empowered, and good about their school and the people in it.

Recently, Ruth Berkowitz and her colleagues (2017) pub-lished a review of research linking school climate to academic achievement. The review showed, over all, that improved cli-mate correlated with increased academic achievement and, in at least some of the studies, with a decline in the achievement gap.

Apparently, one reason for the achievement gap is that rich students tend to believe they "belong" at school and poor stu-dents tend to believe they don't. A concerted effort by teachers and other staff to show that everyone belongs—that everyone is respected, cared for, and welcome—therefore tends to in-crease the participation, and hence the achievement, of eco-nomically poor students more than it does that of wealthier students, thereby reducing the gap.

Closely related to research on school climate is research assessing the value of "inquiry-based teaching." This is a style of teaching that is less top-down than what usually occurs in schools. It is aimed at bringing students' own questions to the forefront and taking students'—all students'—ideas seriously. When done well, it engages all students, including those who would otherwise be the most disengaged. Several studies have indicated that this style of teaching helps previously poor per-formers improve even more than it helps previously high per-formers, and thereby reduces the achievement gap (Marshall & Alston, 2014; Dickinson, 2016).

A One-Year Experiment in Binghamton, New York, with Remarkable Results

A few years ago, David Sloan Wilson—an evolutionary biologist at Binghamton University—conducted, along with colleagues, a remarkable educational experiment. They started
a new public high school, in Binghamton, NY, that would
enroll only the lowest-performing students (Wilson et al.,
2011). Only those students entering ninth or 10th grade who
had failed three or more courses during the previous school
year were eligible. Of the 117 students who qualified, 56 were
randomly assigned to the experimental school, called Rėgents
Academy, and the remainder, comprising the control group,
remained at Binghamton's single public high school.

Wilson and his colleagues designed the school on the basis
of principles derived from evolutionary theory and research,
but, for our purposes, the design can be understood largely
as an attempt to improve school climate. The innovations included group identity-building activities; assembly and coun-
cil meetings involving students and staff together; a school
constitution signed by all students and staff; an attempt by
the principal and every teacher to interact personally and
positively with every student every day; opportunities for ar-
tistic activities (which included a student-painted mural in
the hall); inquiry-based teaching; and an emphasis on coop-
eration and mutual support in the classroom. In response to
students' requests, Friday afternoons were devoted to a Fun
Club, in which students could pursue activities of their own
choosing. Such activities, of course, reduced the total amount

of time that could be spent directly on academic instruction; yet, the school produced remarkable academic results!

The Regents Academy students not only greatly outperformed the control group on the mandated New York state achievement tests at the end of the year, but performed on par with the average for all students at Binghamton High School. At least by this measure, one year at Regents Academy wiped out years of deficit accumulated over prior school years. According to Wilson and his colleagues, the per-student cost of this program was only slightly greater than that for the regular Binghamton High School.

Yet, apparently for bureaucratic reasons having to do with teacher turnover, the program did not continue into a second year. [Sadly, that doesn't surprise me. The history of public education is filled with innovations that were scrapped when they proved to be successful.]

Why Support for Self-Directed Education Could Be the Ultimate Gap Reducer

There is a lesson here. The more rigid, authoritarian, and narrowly task- and test-driven the school program, the greater is the achievement gap between rich and poor. The more friendly, trusting, and empowering the program, the smaller is the gap.

I've heard people argue that Self-Directed Education—the kind of fully trustful, empowering, student-directed education that occurs at Sudbury model schools and Agile Learning Centers—might work for middle and upper class children, but would not work for children from poor families. That argument is premised on the assumption that kids from wealthier families have educationally rich environments at home and therefore don't need coercive schooling, while poor kids don't have such home environments and therefore need coercive schooling in order to learn. But there is good reason to believe that Self-Directed Education, supported by a school or learning center designed for such education, works especially well for poor kids, precisely because it provides the kinds of learning opportunities and support that wealthier kids often have at home.

So far, because there is no public financing for it, relatively few children from poor families are enrolled in schools for Self-Directed Education, and research comparing the effects of such education for poor versus wealthier children is lacking. But my bet is that such schools would greatly reduce and maybe even eliminate the achievement gap, at least to the degree that the gap is not the result of physical insults of poverty, such as malnutrition and lead poisoning. My observation is that kids from poor families are just as curious, just as motivated to learn about the world, and just as motivated to make a good life for themselves as are those from wealthy families. Like all kids, they hunger to take charge of their life and control their own learning; they just need the opportunity. They don't need coercion; they need an environment where they feel welcome, loved, and empowered, and where ample learning opportunities are freely available to all.

Wouldn't it be great if some school system, somewhere,

would conduct such an experiment? The per-student cost in a school for Self-Directed Education is generally much less than that for standard public schools, so this experiment would actually save public money.

References

Berkowitz, R., et al. (2017). A research synthesis of the associations between socioeconomic background, inequality, school climate, and academic achievement. *Review of Educational Research*, 87, 425-469.

Cho, H., et al. (2012). Do reductions in class size raise students' test scores? Evidence from population variation in Minnesota's elementary schools. *Economics of Education Review*, 31(3), 77–95.

Deruy, E. (2016). In wealthier school districts, students are farther apart. *The Atlantic*, May 3, 2016.

Dickinson, K. (2016). An exploratory study of inquiry-based learning to close the achievement gap in high school reading and writing. Doctoral dissertation, Seattle University. Available at ProQuest.

Gray, P. (2013). Schools are good for showing off, not for learning. Freedom to Learn blog at *Psychology Today*, Sept. 19, 2013. https://www.psychologytoday.com/us/blog/freedom-learn/201309/schools-are-good-showing-not-learning

Hoxby, C. M. (2000). The effects of class size on student achievement: New evidence from population variation. *Quarterly Journal of Economics*, 115, 1239–1285.

Jackson, E., & Page, M. E. (2013). Estimating the distributional effects of education reforms: A look at Project STAR. *Economics of Education Review*, 32, 92–103.

Li, W., & Konstantopoulos, S. (2017). Does class-size reduction close the achievement gap? Evidence from TIMSS 2011. *School Effectiveness and School Improvement*, 28, 292-313.

Marshall, J., & Alston, D. (2014). Effective, sustained inquiry-based instruction promotes higher science proficiency among all groups: A 5-year analysis. *Journal of Science Teacher Education* 25, 807-821.

Reardon, S. F. (2012). The widening academic achievement gap between the rich and the poor. *Community Investments*, 24 (2), 19-39.

Schmidt, W. H., et al. (2015). The role of schooling in perpetuating educational inequality: An international perspective. *Educational Researcher*, 44, 371-386.

Tucker, M. (2017). Differences in performance within schools: Why so much greater than in other countries? *Education Week*'s Blog, Sept. 6, 2017. https://blogs.edweek.org/edweek/top_performers/2017/09/differences_in_performance_within_schools_why_so_much_greater_than_in_other_countries_1.html

Wilson, D. S., et al, (2011). A program for at-risk high school students informed by evolutionary science. *PLoS ONE*, 6 (11).

10

Another Example of Less Teaching Leading to More Learning

Delinquent boys made huge academic gains when freed from classroom lessons

SEPTEMBER 26, 2017

Some of the most fascinating experiments in education occurred in the 1920s and '30s, and almost nobody talks about them today. That was an era when progressive ideas about education were in the air. Even public schools were experimenting with the idea that less teaching and more opportunity for self-direction would pay big educational dividends. In an earlier essay in this collection I described an experiment by L. P. Benezet showing the advantage of not teaching any arithmetic before sixth grade. Now here's another bit of education research that nobody today talks about. It was published in 1930 in the academic journal *School and Society* under the title "An Experiment in Self-Directed Education," by Herbert Williams, the teacher who carried out the research.

The practical problem Williams was trying to address was what to do about delinquent boys, who were frequently absent from school and were causing trouble in the community. For the sake of this experiment, he went through the Juvenile Court records for the city with a population of about 300,000 and identified the "worst" boys he could find. To that group the school principals added a few more, whom they considered to be their "most serious problems." He ended up with a group that, in his words, "ranged in age from eight to nearly 16, in IQ from 60 to 120, and included colored, Polish, Hungarians, and native white Americans."

The experiment was begun in January 1924, and lasted until the beginning of June that year. During that period the boys were excused from regular school classes and, instead, were assigned to a special room created for them in a technical school. The room was equipped with desks, blackboards, a large table, and a collection of books, including storybooks, nonfiction works, and textbooks for the various grades. The boys were given standard academic achievement tests in January and again, four months later, in May.

And now, I know no better way to convey what happened than to quote Williams directly:

> "No formal instruction was given. In the beginning of the experiment the children were told to keep busy and refrain from annoying any of the others. This was the only rule that was enforced. Otherwise, they were permitted to occupy themselves as they saw fit. The instructor [Williams] from time to time passed from one to another to

see what was being done. One child might be busily occupied in copying a picture from one of the books; another might be reading a fairy story; another occupied with a problem in arithmetic; another reading a history; others might be looking up places on a geography map; and still others would be studying about some machinery.

"Whenever a child was found manifesting an interest in some particular thing, opportunity and encouragement were given him to develop that interest.... The child with an interest and aptitude for mechanical work was given an opportunity to do this sort of work in the high-school machine shop. The same was true for those interested in automobile mechanics, woodworking, printing and the like. Arrangements were made for recreation at the neighborhood YMCA....

"Each child was told of his accomplishments on the achievement test and encouraged to make up for any deficiencies, but he was not forced to devote his time to these. It was a revelation to the writer how these children turned naturally from one subject to another. A boy might spend an entire day on some book that he was reading. The next day he might devote to arithmetic. One 10-year-old became interested in working square root problems and worked all of these he could find in the arithmetic book. A colored boy became interested in history and read all the histories we could supply. His accounts of interesting historical events kept the entire group keenly interested as he related them. Whenever one of the boys found something in his reading which he felt would prove interesting he was permitted to tell it to the group. However, they were not required to pay attention to the speaker if they wanted to continue what they were doing.

"Many of the boys went to the blackboard to work arithmetic problems, primarily for the activity involved. They made up certain games involving arithmetic processes. . . . For example, two or more boys would start at a given signal to add by seventeens to a thousand. The rivalry was often intense, and for some of the boys the increase in speed and accuracy in the fundamentals was striking. The reports of the various boys on interesting material read would stimulate other boys to read the same thing or something of like nature. It is quite possible, too, that the desire to obtain recognition from their fellows motivated them to do tasks that would not have been otherwise attempted.

"Although a total of twenty-six boys were in attendance in this special experimental group for shorter or longer periods, only thirteen were present for both the January, Form A, and May, Form B, Stanford Achievement Tests. This was due to out-of-school adjustments, transfers and other causes. Social adjustment was given first importance, and completeness of the experimental records was not allowed to prevent placing a boy on a farm, for example, if this met a pressing need."

Here are the results from the achievement tests: Over the four-month period of this experiment, the 13 boys gained an average of slightly over 15 months in language age;14 months in arithmetic; 11 months in reading; 11 months in science; and six months in both history and literature. By the end of the experiment all of these children were above grade level overall. The three boys who showed the least gains were also the three who, for reasons of health or family problems, were most often absent from the group. The average gains for the 10 who were regularly present were 17.4 months for language and arithmetic; 15.8 months for science; and 15.5 months for reading.

In concluding the article, Williams wrote: "The most striking fact is that such marked improvement could and did result from such informal, self-directed activity. The writer was not greatly interested in the educational development of these boys. The problem of social adjustment entirely outweighed it in his estimation. He used the special room merely to get better acquainted with the individual boys and to keep them from violating the compulsory attendance law. Whether they learned reading, arithmetic, geography, history and the other subjects was considered relatively unimportant. . . . It should be remembered, too, that these boys spent less time in the classroom and more in shops and the gymnasium and on the playground than is usually the case. . . . In accounting for this increase in educational achievement the writer can only surmise that . . . a personal interest on the part of the supervisor in each child's home conditions, neighborhood, recreation, health and the like as well as an interest in the child individually may have stimulated the child."

My own suspicion, not mentioned by Williams, is that age mixing also played a role. The boys ranged in age from

8 to almost 16. Self-directed education always works best in age-mixed environments (Gray, 2017). Also, of course, these boys were free to spend as much time as they liked on whatever they were studying, which allowed them to dig much more deeply than is ever possible in a standard classroom; and because they were always free to talk with one another they learned from one another. While regular classrooms are perfectly designed to prevent the development and pursuit of genuine interests, this "classroom" did not prevent such development.

Wouldn't it be great if education authorities would take a look back at some of these old research studies and try repeating them today? Today education authorities seem to think the only solution to educational deficiency is more teaching—more of the same of what already isn't working. But research such as Benezet's and Williams's suggests that the solution might lie in less teaching and more trust.

As regular readers of my essays know, I'm not a fan of standardized academic testing, nor of any sort of school system that sees high scores on such tests as a primary educational goal. In my view (and I suspect Williams's as well), the years that we think of as school years should be devoted to discovering who you are and what you like to do, to developing skills in what you like to do, to acquiring social and emotional competence, and to gaining the confidence that you can learn whatever you want, on your own initiative, at the time you need to know it. That all comes from Self-Directed Education, where young people are free to explore the world in ways that are not dependent at all on a special room with textbooks, nor on encouragement to improve scores on someone else's concept of "achievement." Williams's experiment is, to me, just one more example showing that the kinds of "achievements" that we fret and sweat about in our schools are actually quite easily and painlessly attained by young people who for one reason or another decide to attain them and are free to do so in the ways that work best for them.

References

Gray, P. (2017). Self-directed education—unschooling and democratic schooling. In G. Noblit (Ed.), *Oxford research encyclopedia of education.* New York: Oxford University Press.

Williams, H. D. (1930), Experiment in self-directed education. *School and Society,* 31, 715-718.

CPSIA information can be obtained
at www.ICGtesting.com
Printed in the USA
LVHW080245301020
670257LV00016B/856